Making Sense of the
New Testament

Making Sense of the New Testament

THREE CRUCIAL QUESTIONS

CRAIG L. BLOMBERG

Baker Academic
A Division of Baker Book House Co
Grand Rapids, Michigan 49516

© 2004 by Craig L. Blomberg

Published by Baker Academic
a division of Baker Book House Company
P.O. Box 6287, Grand Rapids, MI 49516-6287
www.bakeracademic.com

Printed in the United States of America

Library of Congress Cataloging-in-Publication Data
Blomberg, Craig
    Making sense of the New Testament / Craig L. Blomberg.
        p.   cm. — (Three crucial questions)
    Includes bibliographical references (p.) and index.
    ISBN 0-8010-2747-0 (paper)
    1. Bible N.T.—Evidences, authority, etc. I. Title. II. 3 crucial
questions.
BS2332.B49 2004
225.1—dc22   2003065338

for George Kalemkarian

with profound gratitude for a friendship
that has surpassed three decades

Contents

List of Abbreviations   9

Preface   11

Introduction   13

1. Is the New Testament Historically Reliable?   17

2. Was Paul the True Founder of Christianity?   71

3. How Is the Christian to Apply
   the New Testament to Life?   107

   Summary   145

   Notes   149

   Subject Index   175

   Scripture Index   183

Abbreviations

AJT	*Asia Journal of Theology*
BBR	*Bulletin for Biblical Research*
Bib	*Biblica*
BSac	*Bibliotheca Sacra*
BTB	*Biblical Theology Bulletin*
EvQ	*Evangelical Quarterly*
ExpT	*Expository Times*
HBT	*Horizons in Biblical Theology*
JBL	*Journal of Biblical Literature*
JR	*Journal of Religion*
JSNT	*Journal for the Study of the New Testament*
JTS	*Journal of Theological Studies*
NovT	*Novum Testamentum*
NTS	*New Testament Studies*
PEQ	*Palestine Exploration Quarterly*
SJT	*Scottish Journal of Theology*
TrinJ	*Trinity Journal*
TynB	*Tyndale Bulletin*
VC	*Vigilae Christianae*
WTJ	*Westminster Theological Journal*

Preface

Many people deserve my thanks for enabling this project to come to completion. Jim Weaver, the former academic books editor for Baker, first approached me about getting involved and was willing to issue me a contract with a due date years into the future, due to my many other commitments. Jim Kinney, the current academic editor, was gracious enough to continue to encourage me to pursue the project, even while he was lining me up to do additional writing further down the road. Michelle Stinson and Jeremiah Harrelson, both recent graduates of Denver Seminary's Masters of Arts in Biblical Studies program, devoted numerous hours of research assistance during the 2001–2 and 2002–3 school years, respectively. Jeanette Freitag, as an assistant to our faculty, helped with the final stages of editing. I am also grateful to the administration and trustees of Denver Seminary for appointing me to a position in the spring of 2002 that has provided a little extra time and significant extra resources to enable me to complete this project, while maintaining a normal teaching load, during the past two academic years.

Many Christian books aim to address a broad cross section of the reading public by presenting their discussions at a level readily understandable by college-educated adults, while recognizing that Christian college and seminary students as well as church leaders and pastors may form their primary readership. Footnotes or endnotes then guide interested readers, and particularly scholars, to more detailed studies. This book aims to do all these things as well. Such works also often refer to the well-read or interested layperson as a kind of "golden mean" of individuals addressed.

At the same time, patterns of reading among the American public sometimes make writers wonder just how many laypersons still fit that description!

One individual who clearly does fit the description is George Kalemkarian. As a young, single man, George devoted many hours a week over several years as a volunteer staff person for a Campus Crusade for Christ chapter at Augustana College in Rock Island, Illinois. My greatest Christian nurture during my college years, from 1973–77, came through that chapter. George not only provided loving leadership and consistent, biblical instruction; he also devoured theological literature and was regularly able to point us to key evangelical Christian scholarship to answer our hard questions. And all this took place, not because he had attended a Christian college or seminary, but because he had studied on his own, in addition to holding down a full-time secular job. George subsequently married a young woman he first met through Crusade, June Stunkel, and they have raised two wonderful daughters in Moline, Illinois, where they remain active in the First United Presbyterian Church. We continue to keep in touch, and George remains one of my staunchest supporters and best friends. It is to him that I therefore dedicate this book, with profound gratitude for three decades of friendship and influence.

Introduction

In recent years, Baker Books has published numerous volumes presenting "three crucial questions" about a particularly controversial biblical or theological topic. Helpful studies have canvassed key issues with respect to the Holy Spirit and charismatic gifts, spiritual warfare, the last days or end-times, women in ministry, and so on. One volume that departs from the format of focusing on a narrowly defined theme is Tremper Longman's *Making Sense of the Old Testament: Three Crucial Questions*.[1] In it, Longman tackles three very broad questions—the "keys to understanding the Old Testament," comparing the God of the Old Testament with the God of the New Testament, and guidance for Christians as to how to apply the Old Testament today.

Because of the popularity of Longman's work, Baker Books approached me about composing a companion volume on the New Testament. But what would be our three questions? Certainly the two largest portions of the New Testament deal with the life of Jesus (the four Gospels) and the ministry of Paul (much of Acts and all of his letters). The first two questions should probably surround the work of these two men. And while the New Testament is not as difficult to apply as the Old Testament, issues of application certainly remain crucial. It was decided, then, to formulate three questions about Jesus, Paul, and application. Now we needed to decide on the specific questions.

Arguably the most controversial aspect of the life of Christ during the past two hundred years, since the rise of modern biblical scholarship, is whether or not the New Testament's portraits of Jesus of Nazareth can be trusted. There are opaque portions of the

Gospels, to be sure, but any reasonably literate person with a good translation of the Bible can quickly recognize that Matthew, Mark, Luke, and John all believed Jesus to be much more than a great teacher, a Jewish rabbi, and a controversial first-century prophet. They believed he was also Israel's long-awaited Messiah or liberator, a divinely sent messenger, even God incarnate. From these convictions came a crucial corollary—all humanity would one day be judged based on their response to this Jesus. His followers could look forward to a new age, inaugurated already in his lifetime but consummated only when he would return from heaven to reign on earth. Christians, as those followers later came to be called, would then experience an eternity of unending happiness in the company of God and each other, while those who rejected Jesus and the New Testament's message about him would spend an eternity separated from God and all things good.

One's assessment of the New Testament's claims about Jesus, from this perspective, is thus the most important issue a person can ever face in this life, despite our world's cultures that would replace it with dozens of other allegedly more pressing concerns. But this line of reasoning presupposes that at least the basic contours of the Bible's portrait of Christ are trustworthy. If Jesus did not make the kinds of claims for himself that the New Testament presents, then we may relegate him to a lesser role in the history of humanity and get on with facing more urgent, current events. One of the three crucial questions for this book to address, therefore, must involve the historical reliability of the New Testament. Or, to phrase the question more precisely, do the apparently historical portions of the New Testament in fact communicate trustworthy history? This means that we must particularly scrutinize the Gospels and Acts, which purportedly provide biographies of Jesus and a history of the first generation of Christianity, respectively. But there are autobiographical reflections in Paul's letters that will have to be considered as well, along with more indirect evidence bearing on questions of history in all the New Testament letters and even in the Book of Revelation.

A closely related crucial question redirects our primary attention from Jesus to Paul. Even if the basic picture of Jesus that the New Testament paints proves trustworthy, his message often sounds quite different from that of the first century's greatest missionary preacher, the apostle Paul. Churches in many times and places throughout Christian history have devoted far more attention to Paul than to Jesus as they have tried to encapsulate the gospel message. Can we reconcile the teaching of these two formative figures? Or did Paul so distort Jesus' message that we must choose one over the other? Was Paul, in fact, the second founder, or perhaps even the true founder of Christianity as it has developed down through the centuries? Our second crucial question must therefore address the continuity and discontinuity between Jesus and Paul as they are depicted in the New Testament. Is it a case of "Jesus versus Paul" or can the two be seen as complementing each other, while still maintaining their distinctive qualities? Obviously, we can address this question only after we have a clear understanding of what both men stood for. By the time we have dealt with these two initial crucial questions, then, we will have had to "make sense" of a large portion of the New Testament.

Because interpretation accomplishes little unless it leads to application, the third crucial question will parallel its counterpart in Longman's volume. How do we apply the New Testament today, especially in cultures far removed in time and space from those of the first-century Mediterranean world in which Jesus and Paul ministered? More precisely, what varying principles emerge for applying the New Testament's diverse literary forms? After all, Jesus' parables are not to be interpreted as straightforward history, nor does narrative material in general yield its lessons in the same way as do more direct commands. And biographies, histories, and letters all differ from apocalyptic literature—the literary genre that the Revelation most closely reflects. What in the world are readers to do today with that collection of visions that at times borders on the bizarre?

There are undoubtedly other sets of "three crucial questions" that could help us make considerable sense of the New Testament, but these should go a long way toward fulfilling that objective. Because the scope of this series of books is comparatively modest, each chapter will rapidly survey huge amounts of terrain without the encumbrance of massive scholarly documentation. But I have tried to supply a reasonably ample number of endnotes per chapter that will allow readers to pursue issues in more detail, where they desire to do so, and that will demonstrate that all of the views I put forward in this work are based on more detailed, meticulous scholarship. Even when I defend views held by a minority of scholars, I believe that these views are based on sound argumentation. The majority, especially when it is biased by very liberal presuppositions, is not always right! Readers should come to the issues with open minds and decide for themselves if my presentations at each point prove persuasive. Let us turn, then, to the New Testament itself and see if we can make sense of it.[2]

CHAPTER 1

Is the New Testament Historically Reliable?

Jesus and Christian origins continue to fascinate the American public. The religion shelves of all major bookstore chains stock numerous titles on these topics. Unfortunately, they range all the way from books written by responsible scholars to works of sheer fiction, foisted on the unsuspecting reader as the latest "true discovery" about the beginnings of Christianity. We may discern three categories of such volumes that lie beyond the mainstream of serious, biblical scholarship.

First, and most disturbing of all, are books based on no genuine historical evidence of any kind. A retired professor of atmospheric science at a major state university becomes enthralled with UFOs and publishes two books about an alleged Aramaic document, found in the Middle East but then (conveniently) lost again, preserved only in German translation by a "UFOlogist," that rewrites the Gospel of Matthew. In this document, Jesus becomes an alien from outer space, visiting earth to teach doctrine similar to modern "New Age" philosophy![1] Or again, a best-selling collection of ancient and more recent Christian fiction, called *The Archko Volume,* purports to release to the public the true accounts of Jesus and early Christianity, without admitting that no responsible historian anywhere believes a shred of its contents to reflect historical fact.[2]

A second category involves the distortion of newly discovered evidence. When the Dead Sea Scrolls were unearthed shortly after World War II, all kinds of sensationalist claims were made for how they would radically rewrite the history of Christian origins. That never happened, but another flurry of fanciful exaggerations emerged in the early 1990s when the last round of very fragmentary documents from Qumran, the site of the Dead Sea sect, was finally published and translated. One of the most famous sets of charges comes from a series of works by the Australian writer Barbara Thiering. She alleges that various characters in the documents that describe the members of the Qumran community, and others in the Jewish world of its day, are code names for John the Baptist, Jesus, and some of his followers![3] There is, however, no reason to suspect that Qumran invented such codes, not least because the vast majority of its documents predate the first century and the birth of Christ. Not surprisingly, Thiering has garnered no significant following among fellow scholars.

Distortions of new discoveries can also come from conservative circles. Carsten Thiede, a German evangelical, has written several recent works arguing that tiny fragments of Greek manuscripts found at Qumran, containing just a few letters each, actually represent verses from the Gospel of Mark. If true, these finds would require a date for that Gospel earlier than that which even conservative scholars have usually defended. Thiede also believes that a copy of Matthew in Greek, long preserved in the Magdalen College, Oxford, library, dates to the mid–first century. But virtually all other scholars who have examined these claims find the equation of the Qumran fragments with Mark in error and the Oxford papyrus to have come from the same codex (or book) to which papyri dating to the 200s, now housed in Paris and Barcelona, belonged.[4] Conservative Christians might wish that Thiede's hypotheses proved likely, but it rightly discredits them in the eyes of others if they try to support highly improbable theses simply for the sake of furthering their apologetic.

The third category brings us even closer to the boundaries of responsible scholarship. There are fully credentialed New Testament scholars on the theological "far left" who do bona fide research, but present their opinions as if they reflected a consensus of scholarship when in fact they represent the "radical fringe." By far the most famous example of this in recent years was the "Jesus Seminar," a group of individuals, mostly New Testament scholars (though many had not specialized in historical-Jesus research), who initially numbered more than two hundred but eventually dwindled to less than fifty, and who courted media attention for their semiannual conferences throughout the late 1980s and 1990s. Voting on every saying and deed attributed to Jesus in the four Gospels, plus the apocryphal *Gospel of Thomas*,[5] the Jesus Seminar concluded that only 18 percent of the sayings and 16 percent of the actions of Jesus in these five documents represented something close to what Jesus really said or did.[6]

These conclusions, however, were virtually determined by the Seminar's presuppositions and method. In a particularly candid listing of these presuppositions, the Seminar explains that miracles cannot happen, so that all of the supernatural events of the Gospels are rejected from the outset, and that Jesus never talked about himself, or about the future, or about final judgment (a topic unworthy of an enlightened teacher).[7] These latter presuppositions go far beyond the anti-supernatural bias of the former, which would conclude that Jesus could not have believed himself to be divine or have predicted the future inerrantly. Instead, they affirm what has been true of no other religious leader in history, namely, that Jesus did not make *any* claims about his identity or speculate *at all* about coming events. And, while it may be true that certain modern liberals cannot stomach the notion of a judgment day when all humanity will be brought to account before God, such a belief was nearly universal in Jesus' world, so it would be astonishing if he did not reflect on the topic.

The Jesus Seminar has now completed its work and disbanded but, at the beginning of the new millennium, a comparable Acts Seminar was formed and initial results published, which suggest that the same flawed approaches are being adopted.[8] Fortunately, it has received far less media attention; one can hope that it will simply fizzle out altogether.

Meanwhile, one of the better-kept secrets from the twenty-first-century public is that the so-called Third Quest for the historical Jesus over the past quarter-century has for the most part been proving more and more optimistic about how much we can know about the founder of Christianity. Ben Witherington's survey of approaches in the mid-1990s offers an excellent overview. Focusing on different portions of the Gospels' portraits and comparing them with the unprecedented quantity of information now available about the first-century Jewish, Greek, and Roman worlds, responsible mainstream New Testament scholars have demonstrated the numerous ways in which Jesus was a Spirit-filled prophet of a coming new age, a social reformer, a wise sage, and a marginalized messiah.[9] Only slightly less intense is a renewed scholarly scrutiny of the apostle Paul, which Witherington has similarly surveyed, including a rehabilitation of the historical value of the Book of Acts, especially those sections that deal with Paul's ministry.[10]

But outside of distinctively evangelical circles, even in mainstream, centrist New Testament scholarship, it is still by no means believed that any substantial majority of the Gospels or Acts is historically accurate. Standard criteria are employed to separate the more historical from the less historical parts.[11] Yet here again, recent studies have suggested that these criteria prove inadequate for what they claim to accomplish. The two most common criteria in Gospels scholarship have become known as "dissimilarity" and "multiple attestation." The dissimilarity criterion accepts as authentic that which sets an event or saying in the Gospels off from both the conventional Jewish world of Jesus' day as well as from subsequent Christianity, since it is then unlikely that any other Jew or Christian would have invented it. The criterion of multiple attestation accepts as more probably historical that which is presented in more than one Gospel or in more than one literary form or source that the Gospels employed. Both of these criteria can point out elements that are securely anchored in the ministry of the historical Jesus, but they cannot logically eliminate items that do not pass the two tests. Jesus overlapped with his Jewish predecessors, while early Christians accurately imitated him in numerous respects. Solitary witnesses may also communicate historical truth. So we need more sophisticated criteria if we are going to challenge details in the Gospels as not reflecting accurate history.[12]

In fact, several scholars have recently developed a four-part criterion that makes it more likely that large swaths of the Gospels are historically *accurate*. N. T. Wright, bishop of Durham, England, and arguably evangelicalism's leading New Testament scholar today, calls it the double dissimilarity and similarity criterion. German scholars Gerd Theissen, Annette Merz, and Dagmar Winter all speak of the criterion of historical plausibility. In each case, it is argued, numerous features in the Gospels simultaneously demonstrate (1) enough continuity with Jewish backgrounds to be credible in an Israelite setting from the first third of the first century; (2) enough discontinuity with conventional Judaism to suggest it would not have been invented by an average Jew; (3) enough continuity with early Christianity to show that Jesus was not uniformly misunderstood by his followers; and (4) enough discontinuity with the early Jesus movement to suggest that one of the first Christians did not invent it. When all *four* of these conditions are fulfilled, we may be very confident that the Gospels present us with accurate information. Wright is more optimistic than the trio of Germans about how much material meets these conditions, but even the writings of the latter accept many of the central themes of the Gospels, certainly many more details than modern, highly skeptical German scholarship usually has acknowledged.[13]

The modest scope of this book prevents me from commenting, even briefly, on each of the central themes or portions of the New Testament data. But I can point to numerous more general features that support a substantial measure of confidence in the historical trustworthiness of the five New Testament books that traditionally have been assumed to present a faithful record of the life of Jesus and the first generation of Christian history—the Gospels of Matthew, Mark, Luke, and John, and the Book of Acts. In doing so, we don our historians' hats and try, for the moment, to bracket Christian belief. We do not want to be guilty of doing what we so sharply criticize the Jesus Seminar for doing, which is to presuppose our conclusions.[14] But even if we limit ourselves to the approaches taken by the classical historians who study other people, events, and institutions from the ancient Jewish, Greek, and Roman worlds, a cumulative case emerges which suggests that the Gospels and Acts are very historically reliable.

Textual Criticism

The standard starting point for investigating the trustworthiness of an ancient document does not deal with the credibility of its contents, per se, but rather asks if we can even be confident we have anything close to what the author of that document originally wrote. In most cases, the oldest copies we have of a given book date from centuries after it was first written. Nor do very many copies of a given book typically exist from the eras before the printing press was invented. For example, there are only nine or ten good manuscripts for Caesar's *Gallic War*, and the oldest derives from nine hundred years after the dates of the events described. Only thirty-five of Livy's 142 books of Roman history survive, and these in about twenty manuscripts, only one of which is as old as the fourth century. Only four and one-half of Tacitus's fourteen books of Roman history have survived, and these in only two manuscripts dating to the ninth and eleventh centuries.[15]

By contrast, the textual evidence for the New Testament from the first centuries after it was written is staggering. Scholars of almost every theological stripe agree that Christian scribes copied the New Testament with extraordinary care, matched only by the accuracy of Jewish scribes copying the Hebrew Scriptures (the Christian Old Testament). In the original Greek alone, more than five thousand manuscripts or manuscript fragments of portions of the New Testament have been preserved from the centuries during which the Bible was copied by hand. The oldest of these is a scrap of papyrus designated $\mathfrak{P}^{52}$ that contains parts of John 18:31–33 and 37–38 and dates from the first third of the second century A.D., no more than forty years after John's Gospel was first written in the 90s. More than thirty papyri date from the late second through early third centuries. Some of these contain large portions of entire New Testament books. One of these covers most of the Gospels and Acts ($\mathfrak{P}^{45}$); another, most of the letters of Paul ($\mathfrak{P}^{46}$). Four very reliable and nearly complete New Testaments date from the fourth ($\aleph$ and B) and fifth centuries (A and C).

All kinds of minor variations distinguish these manuscripts from one another, but the vast majority of these variations involve mere changes in spelling, grammar, and style, or accidental omissions or duplications of letters, words, or phrases. Only about four hundred (less than one per page in an average English translation) have any significant bearing on the meaning of the passage at hand, and the most important variations are usually noted in the footnotes of modern-language translations of the

Bible. The only textual variants that affect more than a sentence or two (and most affect only individual words or phrases) are John 7:53–8:11 and Mark 16:9–20. Neither of these passages very likely reflects what John or Mark originally wrote, though the story in John—about the woman caught in adultery—still stands a fairly good chance of being historically accurate. But overall, 97 to 99 percent of the original Greek New Testament can be reconstructed beyond any reasonable doubt. Moreover, no Christian doctrine is founded solely, or even primarily, on any textually disputed passage.[16]

Thus even the most liberal members of the Jesus Seminar agree with very conservative, evangelical scholars that there is no historical evidence whatsoever to support the claims of some modern-day Mormons or Muslims that the text of the New Testament became so corrupted over the centuries that we have no way of being sure what the original contained. These claims in fact contradict the official teachings of both religions. Joseph Smith's declarations, enshrined in the distinctive, additional Scriptures of the Latter-day Saints, and Islam's holy book, the Qur'an, both refer to the Bible as the Word of God and strongly support the accuracy of its contents, while stopping short of affirming full-fledged inerrancy. But the unofficial teachings of many leaders in both movements have, unjustifiably, often called this accuracy into question.[17]

Authorship and Date

Once we have established that we have a trustworthy reconstruction of what an ancient document contained, based on the comparison of the manuscripts that exist from a later date, we are ready to begin to assess the truthfulness of its contents. The next standard question for historians of antiquity is if we can determine the author of the document and the date at which it was written. If the author turns out to be someone who was in a position to know the facts about the people or the events described, if we can determine that his or her character was generally trustworthy, our conviction about the reliability of the document increases. If the date at which the work was written was within the lifetime of eyewitnesses of the events narrated, our confidence similarly rises. If these conditions are not fulfilled, we become more skeptical about the contents of the history that is narrated.

How do the Gospels and Acts fare when tested by these criteria? Remarkably well, at least by ancient standards. Strictly speaking, the authors of these five books are anonymous, since the names Matthew, Mark, Luke, and John do not appear in any verse as the writers of these documents. The names do appear, however, in all the existing manuscripts as titles to the four Gospels. Yet it is unlikely that four early Christians independently decided to call their writings "The Gospel according to X" (where "X" stands for the name of the author). It is more probable that the early church added these parallel titles to distinguish one Gospel from the next when they were first combined to form a fourfold collection.[18]

On the other hand, among the many Christian writers from the second through fourth centuries who commented on New Testament origins, no other names besides Matthew, Mark, Luke, or John were ever put forward as possible authors of the Gospels and Acts. The earliest of these writers, Papias, was a disciple of the apostle John and wrote in the early second century, just one generation after the death of that last apostle. A consideration of everything Papias claimed about the Gospels lies beyond our scope here, and there are certain statements of his that appear less than fully reliable.[19] But would the early church uniformly have ascribed the first three Gospels and Acts to Matthew, Mark, and Luke without believing them to have been their true authors? After all, the later second- through fifth-century apocryphal Gospels and Acts were all (falsely) ascribed to highly reputable, influential early Christians to try to make them appear as authoritative and credible as possible. Thus we have Gospels supposedly written by Peter and James, Thomas and Philip, Bartholomew and Matthias (the replacement for Judas who betrayed Jesus), and even Nicodemus and Mary. Similarly, apocryphal Acts appear in the names of Andrew, John, Peter, Paul, and Thomas.[20]

In comparison, Mark and Luke are far more obscure characters in the pages of the New Testament. Mark appears nowhere by name in the Gospels; in Acts he is best known as the traveling companion of Paul and Barnabas who deserted them on their first missionary journey (Acts 13:13). Luke appears only in the closing greetings in three of Paul's letters, from which we also learn that he was a doctor (Col. 4:14; cf. also 2 Tim. 4:11, Philem. 24). Neither was one of the twelve "apostles"; both prove unlikely candidates for an ascription of authorship unless they actually wrote the documents attributed to them (in Luke's case, both the Gospel that bears his name and the Acts of the Apostles). Matthew *was* one of the Twelve but, as a former tax collector working (indirectly) for the hated Romans, he would have been the most notorious from an orthodox Jewish perspective. Like Simon the Zealot (at the opposite end of the political spectrum, violently opposed to Rome), Matthew would not have been one of the first nine or ten disciples to be chosen if one were trying to lend authority or credibility to a fictitious document written by someone else.

John, on the other hand, was one of the inner core of three disciples (with his brother James and Peter) who were privy to experiences in Jesus' life that the rest were not. An apocryphal Acts is attributed to him, as we have noted, and Papias's testimony is unclear as to whether he thought it was John the apostle who authored the Gospel bearing his name or a different John, called the elder, who was a second-generation follower of the apostle. But the question for which no good answer has ever emerged, if the author of "John" were not the son of Zebedee and apostle by that name, is why does this writer (unlike the Synoptists—Matthew, Mark, and Luke) always refer to John the Baptist merely as "John" and expect his audience to know which John was in view? And the apparent self-reference by the author of this Gospel, five times referring to "the beloved disciple," comports well with one who belonged to Jesus' inner circle (see John 13:23–25; 19:26–27, 34–35; 20:2–5, 8; 21:1–7, 20–22).[21]

Liberal New Testament scholars today tend to put Mark a few years one side or the other of A.D. 70, Matthew and Luke–Acts sometime in the 80s, and John in the 90s. As for dating, all of these documents are quoted or alluded to in early-second-century Christian writings, so they can scarcely be dated to later than the first century. Explicit statements combined with reasonable inferences from the various "Church Fathers" lead most conservative scholars, however, to locate all three Synoptic Gospels plus Acts in the 60s with John still in the 90s.[22]

The internal evidence of these five books meshes well with the earlier dates. A completely convincing account of the abrupt end of Acts has never been given, unless Luke was writing shortly after the events with which the book concludes. Why else would he spend more than a quarter of his account narrating the arrest, imprisonment, trials, and appeal of Paul (chaps. 21–28) and then leave us hanging with Paul's two-year period of house arrest in Rome awaiting the results of his appeal, unless Luke was writing before he knew what those results were? But if this logic proves compelling, then he must have written Acts in about A.D. 62, since we know from other ancient sources that Festus came to power in Judea in 59. And we know from Acts that Paul appealed to the emperor shortly after Festus's accession and that he spent the subsequent winter shipwrecked on the island of Malta and the next two years in Rome.[23]

We may then infer that the Gospel of Luke was written before the Acts of the Apostles, since the latter forms the sequel to the former. Because most modern scholars believe Luke relied in part on Mark's Gospel, Mark must be dated even earlier. Perhaps all three of these works were written, then, in the early 60s. According to Irenaeus, who wrote toward the end of the second century, Matthew compiled his account "while Peter and Paul were preaching the gospel and founding the church in Rome" (*Against Heresies* 3.1.1). This also requires a date no later than the mid-60s, after which both Christian leaders lost their lives in Nero's persecution of the church (A.D. 64–68).

The point to be stressed, however, is that on *either* the more liberal set of dates *or* the more conservative one, the Gospels and Acts were written in the first century. Those that were not written by eyewitnesses of the life of Christ like Matthew and John were written by people in a position to interview those eyewitnesses— Mark and Luke. This statement also holds true even if we adopt the more skeptical approach that these documents were originally anonymous, following the standard liberal assumption that the authors were second-generation Christian followers of the apostles. Furthermore, we must remember that first-century Christianity faced numerous opponents who would have delighted in refuting the claims of this fledgling religion. What better way to do that than to declare that the Gospels and Acts simply did not tell the story accurately? As long as hostile eyewitnesses to the life of Christ and the formation of the church were still living, such a rebuttal was always possible. But there is no record anywhere that anyone ever made such a charge. In fact the earliest and most enduring charge that non-Christian Jews made against Christianity's claims, beginning already during Christ's life, tacitly admitted the truthfulness of its historical records (see below, p. 48).

Today, thirty to sixty years between a series of events and the historical records that narrate them seems like a long time. If Jesus was crucified in around A.D. 30, and the earliest Gospel was written in the 60s and the latest in the 90s, surely considerable distortion could have developed even during this period of time. Part of our response to this allegation comes later in this chapter (see pp. 33–36). Here two comments are in order. First, there is reason to believe that Matthew, Mark, Luke, and John used earlier written sources, shorter than an entire Gospel, in researching and writing at least portions of their books. These earlier sources may be dated to as early as the 50s. The identical wording of numerous sayings of Jesus, translated from his original Aramaic into Greek, found jointly in the Gospels of Matthew and Luke but not in Mark, suggests their dependence on a common source other than Mark.[24] Less certain but still quite possible is John's use of a "signs source," often dated to the 60s, for his distinctive miracle stories, in this case because of a unique style perceptible in parts of these narratives. Interestingly, even the Jesus Seminar accepts both of these hypotheses as probable, thereby cutting in half the period of time they believe many of the words and deeds of Jesus circulated before being compiled in some kind of written documents (from A.D. 30–50 versus 30–70 or 80 for the Synoptics, and from 30–60 versus 30–90 for John).[25]

Second, even sixty years between a set of events and a written history about them is a remarkably short period of time by ancient standards. The largely legendary sagas of early Greek and Roman heroes circulated by word of mouth for centuries, at times for more than a millennium, before being written down. Even the relatively sober biographies of Alexander the Great, for example, that are still in existence date from the late first and early second centuries A.D. Yet Alexander died in 323 B.C., so there is a gap of about five hundred years before his biographers Plutarch and Arrian wrote their books about his life. Both writers, however, acknowledge copious indebtedness to previous written sources, and classical historians believe they can derive in great detail accurate historical information about Alexander from these works, while at the same time recognizing they are by no means flawless.[26] The oft-cited quotation by the Roman historian A. N. Sherwin-White of a generation ago still sums up the irony surrounding contemporary skepticism: "So, it is astonishing that while Graeco-Roman historians have been growing in confidence, the twentieth-century study of the Gospel narratives, starting from no less promising material, has taken so gloomy a turn. . . ."[27]

The Genres of the Gospels and Acts

Everything we have said thus far presupposes that the four Evangelists thought they were writing relatively straightforward history and biography. That is certainly what the Gospels and Acts appear to be presenting, and it is the dominant way readers have understood these works throughout church history. But is this presupposition accurate? What are the closest parallels in the literature of the ancient Mediterranean world to these documents, and what can we learn from attempts to label their literary form or genre? Various efforts have been made in modern biblical criticism to declare these works largely fictitious on the basis of alleged parallels with myth, legend, romance, and the like. For the better part of the twentieth century, a majority of critics declared their genre to be *sui generis* (i.e., one of a kind or, literally, their "own genre").[28] But a majority of recent specialized studies has recognized that the closest parallels are found among the comparatively trustworthy histories and biographies of writers like the Jewish historian Josephus, and the Greek historians Herodotus and Thucydides.[29] Particularly instructive are the prefaces to Luke and Acts (Luke 1:1–4; Acts 1:1–2), which not only parallel the prefaces in the works of these non-Christian historians but also describe Luke relying on previous sources, eyewitness interviews, and reliable oral tradition. While the attempt to prove that Luke was a doctor, based on allegedly distinctive medical vocabulary, was abandoned almost a century ago, Loveday Alexander has demonstrated that the closest parallels to Luke's language appear in Greco-Roman "technical prose," which she broadly defines as "scientific" literature, including treatises on such topics as medicine, philosophy, mathematics, engineering, and rhetoric.[30] Such parallels again distance the biblical writers from the most overtly fictitious literature of their day and inspire confidence that concern for accuracy was one of the central characteristics of the composition of the Gospels and Acts.

The Gospel of John, of course, is more unlike than like the Synoptics in the details of Jesus' life it presents, including the linguistic style of Jesus' speech. Not surprisingly, scholars have questioned whether the Fourth Gospel may be identified by the same genre, and whether it proves to be as accurate, as Matthew, Mark, and Luke. The purpose statement for the Fourth Gospel appears in John 20:31: "But these [things] are written that you may believe that Jesus is the Messiah, the Son of God, and that by believing you may have life in his name." This statement could suggest that John's concern to promote Christian faith has overridden his concern for historical accuracy. But then one must ask if largely fictitious literature would have promoted such faith, when others in John's world could have debunked his narrative. Elsewhere it is clear that one of John's dominant concerns is "truth" (see esp. 19:35; 21:24). It is hard to imagine that he would have thought a largely falsified narrative would help people to believe the truth at any level, historical or theological.[31] The reason John includes episodes largely different from the Synoptics is probably because he recognized that his audiences (the churches in and around Ephesus) already knew a fair portion of that material well through his previous preaching ministry among them.[32] John's distinctive style is clearly his own. But the very reason he gives for feeling free to write up Jesus' teachings more in his own words than Matthew, Mark, and Luke do—namely, the inspiration of the Holy Spirit (John 14:26)—is a key reason for believing John nevertheless preserved the gist of Jesus' teachings accurately. On a spectrum of ancient works ranging from highly objective chronicles of history to totally fictitious works, John perhaps falls just slightly farther away from the former end than do the Synoptics, but the first three Gospels still remain the closest literary parallels to John in antiquity.[33]

What often leads modern readers astray is that contemporary

conventions for writing history and biography usually require standards of precision that people had not even invented, much less begun to follow, in the ancient world. In cultures that had yet to create any symbol corresponding to our quotation mark, or to feel any need for one, it was perfectly appropriate to rephrase someone else's language in one's own words, so long as one was faithful to the "gist" or intention of the original speaker. It was considered not only appropriate but also necessary to abridge or abbreviate long accounts, to insert one's own commentary into the text (as parenthetical remarks in a world without symbols for parentheses), and to be highly selective as to what one narrated about a given person or event.[34] Today we would feel a biography was deficient if it did not narrate something about the birth and upbringing of an individual or if it spent nearly half of its time describing the events immediately preceding that person's death. The same would be true if it rearranged key events of a person's life topically, rather than following strict chronology. Yet when Mark and John do precisely these things, they are following good ancient Mediterranean precedent. The "Lives of the Philosophers" compiled by Diogenes Laertius in the early third century often look very much like the canonical Gospels in this respect. When one recalls that Christians believed the most significant feature of Jesus' life was his death (for the sins of the world), their choice of emphasis makes good sense.

With respect to Acts, much scholarly study has surrounded its speeches. On the one hand, critics sometimes complain that the core message of every speech is the same, irrespective of the speaker. Luke, they allege, must have created a "one-size-fits-all" prototype and indiscriminately attributed it to every early Christian preacher. On the other hand, the critics also observe the extraordinary variation of specific details from one speech to the next, and so again attribute the variety to Luke's creation. Surely the same speaker, for example Paul, would not have so varied his messages from one occasion to the next.

In fact, these two criticisms largely cancel each other out! What the combination of unity and diversity in the preaching of Acts demonstrates is how perfectly tailored each message is to its particular audience. Paul and Peter may both resemble each other when speaking to the same kinds of audiences, as in the Jewish temple or synagogues (cf., e.g., Acts 3:12–26 with 13:16–48). But Paul will sound quite different speaking to pagans in Lystra for whom the Old Testament and fulfillment of Jewish hopes would have meant nothing (14:15–18)! Still, the core commonalities—the centrality of the resurrection of Jesus and the need to repent of sin to receive forgiveness and the indwelling Holy Spirit—show that there is a unity to the early Christian message that transcends any specific context.[35]

The Success of the Evangelists' Enterprise

One may grant that Matthew, Mark, Luke, and John thought they were writing good history and biography by the standards of their day. But how successful were they? Those who answer this question negatively often base their opinion on any or all of the following three allegations.

HISTORICAL INTEREST?

To begin, it is often argued that the first generation of Christians would not have been terribly interested in preserving an accurate historical record of their origins. Three lines of reasoning at first glance appear to support this claim. First, it is alleged that early Christian prophets spoke in the name of the risen Lord what they believed God was telling the churches through them, and that these words would have become intermingled with the teachings of the historical Jesus. After all, it was the same person speaking on both occasions, and Greco-Roman oracles seem to have adopted a similar practice. Second, the first generation of Christianity clearly entertained a lively hope in the end of the world, brought about by the return of Christ, within its lifetime. Who would be around to read a history of their movement anyway? Finally, the ideological bias of the authors—a passionate commitment to Christian theology—would have inevitably skewed their accounts. We must consider each of these charges in turn.

With regard to Christian prophecy, irrespective of possible analogies in other religions of the day, the only actual hard data we have in the New Testament contradict the charge that the words of Jesus during his lifetime were mixed together with what later Christians believed he was saying to the churches. The three actual references in which we learn the contents of first-century Christian prophecy all clearly distinguish their words from those of the historical Jesus. Twice in Acts, Agabus appears on the scene to prophesy—the first time about a coming famine in Judea, the second time about Paul's imminent imprisonment in Jerusalem (Acts 11:28; 21:11). Once in Revelation, we are told that John's specific words to local churches were given to him as prophecy (Revelation 2–3 as the outgrowth of 1:3). Nowhere in the Gospels do any of these sayings appear as though Jesus had said them during his lifetime. The hypothesis to the contrary proves groundless.[36]

With respect to the belief that the world could end at any time, it is important to observe that this was not a new conviction unique to Christians. Jews from the eighth century B.C. onward had heard a succession of prophets declare that the Day of the Lord was at hand (e.g., Joel 2:1; Obad. 14; Hab. 2:3). Yet centuries passed, the world continued to exist in its current form, and Jews inscribed the preaching of those same prophets in books that would form part of their biblical canon. In the intertestamental period, Psalm 90:4 became a favorite text to explain how Judaism could still believe in an imminent judgment day: "[A] day with the Lord is as a thousand years."[37] What seems long from a human perspective is very brief from God's eternal perspective. Moreover, the Essene sect at Qumran that has given us the Dead Sea Scrolls harbored as vivid a hope as any Jewish group for God's imminent, apocalyptic intervention into this world to punish his enemies and vindicate his followers. Yet the Essenes produced more literature, including works that enable scholars today to chart the history of their community, than any other Jewish group that we know of in pre-Christian times. Given that all of the first Christians were originally Jews, it is doubtful that a conviction that Jesus might return in their lifetime would keep them from being interested in chronicling their history.

As for the notion that a strong ideological commitment necessarily leads to the falsification or distortion of historical records, in fact at times the opposite is true. There is no question that a special agenda can skew the facts, but in certain instances the very ideological commitments that lead to recording a certain portion of history require that one tell the story straight. Consider the example of Jewish historians after the Nazi holocaust in the mid–

twentieth century. Precisely *because* of their passionate concern that such atrocities never again befall their people (or anyone else), Jewish chroniclers carefully collected and published detail after detail about the horrors their people experienced, culminating in the death of six million. Conversely, it was certain later non-Jewish writers, not personally involved in the events of World War II, that generated the "revisionist" accounts falsely alleging that a far smaller number of victims had been involved.

The practice of the New Testament writers closely parallels this example of modern, Jewish historians. What distinguished Jewish and Christian claims from those of all other religions in the ancient Mediterranean world was the belief that God had acted uniquely in history through real and recent human beings to provide salvation for humanity. What distinguished Christianity from its Jewish roots was the claim that the decisive, once-for-all sin offering was provided by the crucifixion of the man Jesus of Nazareth, who was subsequently vindicated by God through his bodily resurrection from the grave. If these claims are not historically accurate, Christianity collapses.[38] Therefore the very theology that the skeptics claim would have warped the New Testament accounts more likely acted as a safeguard against such distortion. What is more, as far as we can tell, the ancients never wrote history without some ideological lens through which events were viewed. Their attitude, in essence, was to ask what point there was in recording history if people could not learn certain lessons from it. At the same time, contrary to the claims of some modern scholars, they could distinguish good from bad history, even granted propagandistic purposes (see esp. Lucian's *On Writing History*).[39]

ABILITY TO WRITE HISTORY?

One may grant that the first followers of Jesus would have been interested in writing a history of the foundation of their movement. But then a second question arises. Were they *able* to write reliable history? Even if we accept the conservative dates for the Synoptics and Acts (the 60s) and recognize that these books relied on even earlier written sources, eyewitness testimony, and oral tradition, thirty years seems like a long time for everything to have been preserved intact. Bart Ehrman speaks for many skeptics when he likens the process to the children's game of "telephone."[40] Take a room full of a couple dozen people, whisper a fairly lengthy and complicated statement to the first person, have them whisper to the next person what they heard and remembered, and continue the process until the message has been "transmitted" to the last person in the room. When that person is then asked to repeat the initial message out loud for everyone to hear, it is usually hilarious because it has become so garbled. How in the world can we seriously imagine Christians preserving throughout the entire Roman Empire for a whole generation the enormous number of details we find in the Gospels and Acts?

The simplest answer to this question is that the process of transmitting information about Jesus and the early church bore little resemblance to the uncontrolled behavior of children playing "telephone." The first-century Roman Empire contained only oral cultures. All important information circulated by word of mouth. A majority of the people living in the empire were illiterate. Jewish men had a much higher literacy rate than the rest of the populace because many of them had attended school in local synagogues from age five to about twelve or thirteen. They would have learned enough to be able to read the Hebrew Scriptures, but few could have ever afforded their own copies. So education took place, as it did also in the larger Greco-Roman world, by rote memorization. Many Jewish men had sizable chunks of what we call the Old Testament committed to memory. Would-be rabbis, who underwent additional training during their teenage years as pupils of revered Jewish teachers, in some instances learned the entire Scriptures. There are even accounts of scribes completing a copy of the Old Testament and then having a respected rabbi proofread it by checking it against the version he had memorized! Boys who had access to education in the Greco-Roman world at times learned part or all of Homer's *Iliad* and *Odyssey* by heart. In this kind of culture, committing the contents of a book as small as a Gospel to memory would have been comparatively easy, especially when we observe that 80 to 90 percent of Jesus' teachings are couched in poetic form.[41]

The countercharge may then be raised, however, that we do not have four Gospels that are word-for-word identical. Memorization may account for some of the similarities, though we have already noted that literary dependence of one Gospel on another or on a common source probably explains the majority of texts in which identical wording occurs. But what of all the differences? One of the answers to this question involves a second dimension to the memorization customs of the ancient Middle East. Sacred traditions passed along *solely* by word of mouth were recounted, sometimes even sung, by storytellers in small villages where the people often gathered around a fire after dark, after supper, in an environment (minus electricity) with little else to do. In these situations, not least to maintain interest in well-known tales, any given storyteller had the right to omit or include, to expand or abbreviate, and to provide commentary on the various details of the stories. But this flexibility in transmission had specific limits. Fixed points in every story, without which the accounts could not be properly understood, had to be preserved accurately, and it was the responsibility of the community to interrupt and correct a storyteller if these were not properly presented. In most instances, a given "performance" varied anywhere from 10 to 40 percent from the previous one. Interestingly, this is very similar to the amounts that one of the Synoptic Gospels varies from another, wherever two or more recount the same episode. So we probably need to feature "developments in the oral tradition" alongside literary copying and theological editing as a significant component in the formation of the Gospels as we know them.[42]

Two other elements in early Christian oral tradition set it off sharply from Ehrman's "telephone" analogy. First, there is evidence that rabbis permitted private note-taking after public teaching to facilitate learning and memorization. Although the notion has been lampooned, it is not at all unreasonable to imagine some of Jesus' disciples scribbling notes to themselves after a day of exposure to his teaching ministry in order to help them remember its highlights. Something quite like that seems to have been the process utilized at Qumran to preserve the teachings of their anonymous "Teacher of Righteousness."[43] Second, the pattern of Peter, John, and James in Acts and the epistles of initiating travels or calling meetings to check up on the arrival of the gospel in a new geographical location shows that the early church wanted to ensure the accuracy of what was preached or taught (see esp. Acts 8, 15, 21; Galatians 1–2). The fledgling church was not the amorphous, free-wheeling entity as it is often portrayed but rather a "purpose-driven" community with an acknowledged leadership and mechanisms of accountability.[44]

ACCURACY IN THE FINAL PRODUCT?

We have seen that the writers of the Gospels and Acts most likely would have been interested in preserving biographies of Jesus and a history of the first generation of Christianity. We have observed that all the mechanisms were in place in their world for them to have done so with a high degree of accuracy. The final question in this series that now must be addressed is, "But did they succeed in this enterprise?" As one compares the four Gospel accounts where they run parallel, or as one tries to fit the information of Acts together with the historical information found in Paul's epistles, do we find harmony or disunity? Certainly long lists of supposed contradictions here and elsewhere in the Bible have been drawn up.[45] Aren't these enough to disprove claims of historical trustworthiness irrespective of the more general arguments presented thus far?

The Four Gospels

The only fully adequate way to answer this question would be to look at each alleged contradiction one at a time, which would result in a much larger book. I have elsewhere surveyed virtually all of the most famous supposed contradictions both among the Synoptics and between the Synoptics and John and refer the reader to those fuller treatments.[46] A sizable majority of the apparent discrepancies disappear once we recall the freer standards of historical reportage in the ancient world (see above, p. 30). But even our modern, scientific world preserves similar conventions. No one thinks to accuse the news reporter of an error when he or she declares, "President so-and-so announced today that . . . ," when in fact it was his press secretary who read a document produced by a script writer and presumably run past the president, however briefly. So we should scarcely be surprised when Matthew telescopes the account of the Gentile centurion requesting a miracle from Jesus via Jewish intermediaries (so Luke 7:6) into one in which the centurion himself comes with the request (Matt. 8:5). Acting through an intermediary could be spoken of as acting for oneself.

Numerous other examples could be given. Was the Last Supper celebrated on the night of the Passover meal (so apparently Mark 14:12–16) or before it (so apparently John 18:28 and 19:14)? Probably it was on the Passover, since John 18:28 seems to allude to the weeklong Passover festival, while 19:14 can be taken as the Day of Preparation *for the Sabbath* during Passover week (as in the NIV). Did Jesus send the demons into the swine in Gerasa (Mark 5:1; Luke 8:26) or in Gadara (Matt. 8:28)? Probably it was near Khersa—a city on the east bank of the Sea of Galilee, which spelled in Greek could easily yield Gerasa—in the *province* of Gadara.[47] The important point to make here is that none of these problems is new. The early church fathers, writing in the second through sixth centuries, studied the New Testament closely enough to recognize all the apparent discrepancies in the text that modern critics emphasize. Augustine's famous fifth-century commentary, entitled *Harmony of the Gospels,* deals with a large number of them. Today, virtually any detailed evangelical commentary on one of the four Gospels or Acts will include possible solutions to these problems in its passage-by-passage exposition. Not all harmonizations prove equally convincing, and many "contradictions" have more than one plausible resolution. But the point is that thoughtful men and women throughout church history, fully aware of these problems, have also recognized that none of them needs to undermine one's confidence in the Bible's trustworthiness. Too often modern skeptics make it sound as if we know something today that our predecessors did not that *now* makes belief in the historical reliability of Scripture untenable. That claim is simply false.

In fact, what *has* changed are many scholars' attitudes toward harmonization. As noted above (p. 28), classical historians are far more confident about our ability to retrieve historical facts from ancient documents, even when they appear to contain minor contradictions, than many biblical scholars are. An excellent example of this comes from the work of the Canadian historian Paul Merkley. Julius Caesar's crossing of the Rubicon River as he returned from Gaul to Italy in 49 B.C. is often put forward as one incontrovertible fact of Roman history that also had *historic* significance. With that action, Caesar committed himself to civil war and the course of the Roman republic was forever altered; it would become an empire instead. What is often not mentioned is that we do not know for sure the exact date or location of this crossing. Moreover, as with the Gospels, we have four accounts of the event from later historians—Velleius Paterculus, Plutarch, Suetonius, and Appian. Only the first of these four men was born before the mid–first century *after* Christ. All claim to have relied on one eyewitness source, that of Asnius Pollio, whose works have entirely disappeared. The four accounts vary to approximately the same degree as the Gospels do when they overlap in content. Suetonius even introduces a miracle into his account, claiming that Caesar's decision was triggered because he saw "an apparition of superhuman size and beauty" that was "sitting on the river bank, playing a reed pipe." Yet Caesar's crossing of the Rubicon continues to be cited as one of the most well-established historical facts of antiquity. A similar confidence should be transferred to the four Gospels, which remain much closer in time and access to the events they narrate.[48]

I have elsewhere pointed out how historians of the life of Alexander the Great, as well as students of Josephus who compare his various writings about a given person or event, regularly adopt a cautious form of harmonization of apparently discrepant details. Just because *some* harmonizations prove implausible does not mean the entire method should be discarded. For example, it is unlikely that the solution to the Synoptics' varying locations of Jesus healing the blind men near Jericho (as Jesus was "leaving" the city—Mark 10:46; Matt. 20:29—or as he was "approaching" the city—Luke 18:35) is resolved by postulating two separate Jerichos, one the Old Testament site that lay in ruins, and the other the New Testament town, as has sometimes been suggested. No first-century listener would assume that an uninhabited town from centuries past would be in view when a narrator spoke simply of "Jericho." The Greek expression translated "approaching" may simply mean "being in the vicinity of."[49] On the other hand, only Matthew speaks of Jesus healing *two* blind men in this narrative (Matt. 20:30–34). But neither Mark nor Luke claims that there was *only* one person present, so it is natural to imagine that these two Gospel writers, or the oral tradition they inherited, had simply streamlined the account and spoken of the one who most directly interacted with Jesus and whose name was preserved—Bartimaeus. This kind of "additive" harmonization is common in scholarly studies of other ancient characters.[50]

But what of the much larger differences between the Synoptics and John? Again I will have to refer the reader to my much fuller discussion of this matter in an entire book on the topic.[51] But we can make a few broad generalizations here. First, at the risk of stating the obvious, one of the reasons John seems so different is because he is not directly dependent on one or more of the Synoptics in the same way that Luke and Matthew depend on Mark. Had the four Evangelists all written entirely independently of each other, there might have been as much diversity in selection of detail among the Synoptics as there now is between the Synoptics and John. Even though he uses hyperbole, John's closing comment that "Jesus did many other things as well," so that "if every one of them were written down, I suppose that even the whole world would not have room for the books that would be written," surely applies to all major, complex, and influential figures of history. If we did not have *three* so similar Gospels, the differences between John and any *one* of them would not stand out so starkly.

Second, and closely related to this point, we must remember how much John and the Synoptics have in common and not focus merely on the differences. A partial list would include

1. the portrait of John the Baptist as fulfillment of Isaiah 40:3 and the forerunner of the Messiah;
2. the contrast between John's baptism with water and the Messiah's coming baptism with the Spirit;
3. the Spirit's anointing of Jesus as testified by the Baptist;
4. the feeding of the five thousand;
5. the walking on the water;
6. the command to a paralytic to "take up your bed and walk";
7. the healing of a Gentile official's son at a distance;
8. miraculous healings that break the Sabbath laws against working on that day;
9. Jesus' refusing to work miracles merely to satisfy his opponents;
10. failed attempts to arrest Jesus prematurely;

11. Jesus' friendship with reflective Mary and bustling Martha;
12. Jesus' insistence on the need for new, spiritual birth;
13. the promise of an abundant harvest for spiritual farmers;
14. the rejection of a prophet in his homeland;
15. judgment by works for unbelievers;
16. the Father revealing the Son and no one fully knowing the Father but the Son;
17. Jesus and his disciples as "the light of the world";
18. Jesus' teaching functioning in part to harden the hearts of those who have already rejected him, fulfilling Isaiah 6:9–10;
19. Jesus as the good shepherd;
20. true discipleship as servanthood;
21. Jesus resisting temptation to abandon the road to the cross;
22. receiving Jesus as receiving the One who sent him;
23. a disciple as no greater than his master;
24. the promise that the Holy Spirit will tell Jesus' followers what to say in the future;
25. coming expulsion of believers from Jewish synagogues;
26. the expelled believers' dispersion around the known world; and
27. the disciples given the authority to forgive or retain the sins of others.[52]

And the list could be lengthened.

Third, the unique circumstances that led to the composition of the Fourth Gospel account for John's choice to narrate largely different episodes from Christ's life. Combining the internal and external evidence, it appears that John was written at the end of the first century to the collection of house congregations in and around Ephesus, to combat twin challenges that the church in that community was facing. On the one hand, the Gnostic teacher Cerinthus had gained followers from among the Christians there, promoting, among other things, a "docetism" that accepted Jesus' deity but denied his humanity. The numerous references throughout John's Gospel to Jesus' truly becoming flesh, having emotions, eating and drinking, being subordinate to his Father, and doing nothing but carrying out his Father's will, which finally included dying an excruciating and fully human death, all undoubtedly are included to combat this theological error. On the other hand, by the end of the first century the separation between church and synagogue was largely complete, and that largely because the Jewish leaders had excommunicated their own people who professed belief in Jesus as Messiah. So a high percentage of the passages unique to John involve Jesus preaching to or disputing with Jewish leaders to justify his actions and claims. Reading these stories would encourage Jewish Christians that they had indeed made the right choice by following Jesus and would also give them evangelistic "ammunition" in dealing with their unsaved Jewish friends and family.[53]

Fourth, there are numerous fascinating examples of "interlocking" between John and the Synoptics, in which an episode or statement in the Synoptics makes sense only if one has information unique to John, and vice versa. For example, John 3:24 makes passing reference to a time "before John was put in prison," yet nowhere else in John's Gospel does any reference to this imprisonment appear. Presumably John was assuming his audience had at least heard of that event, as narrated in Mark 6:14–29 and parallels. Or again, in his account of Jesus' trials, John almost totally omits Christ's climactic appearance before the Sanhedrin, presided over by Caiaphas. Yet he makes two passing remarks that show that he knows of that event, when he writes, "Then Annas sent him, still bound, to Caiaphas the high priest" (John 18:24), and "Then the Jews led Jesus from Caiaphas . . ." (v. 28). Again, John must be able to assume that his audience knew the story (it appears in all the Synoptics—Mark 14:53–65 and parallels). Meanwhile, John is interested in describing a preliminary hearing before the previous high priest, Caiaphas's father-in-law, Annas (John 18:13, 19–23).

In other instances, the interlocking works in the reverse direction. Readers of only the Synoptic Gospels might wonder why the Jewish leaders had to send Jesus to the Roman governor, Pontius Pilate (Mark 15:1–3 par.). If they had found Jesus guilty of blasphemy, why didn't they just stone him according to their Law? Only John provides the answer: the Jewish leaders under Rome

were not permitted to carry out the death penalty in such cases
(John 18:31). Similarly, those reading only Matthew, Mark, and
Luke might wonder if Jesus' first disciples actually left their occupations instantly to follow him the very first time he ever set eyes
on them. Mark 1:16–20 and parallels could certainly be taken that
way, without any additional information. But John 1:35–42 makes
clear that several of the apostles first met Jesus while they were
followers of John the Baptist. They would have witnessed his baptism, become familiar with his ministry, and then later responded
to a more formal call to be one of twelve who literally went on the
road with Jesus.[54]

The Book of Acts

Finally, we consider a different kind of supposed contradiction—
in the Book of Acts. Because the narrative of Luke's second volume contains a lot of information about Paul's preaching, it is
often alleged that the theological emphases that emerge from his
speeches (or sermons) in Acts do not fit well with the major
themes of the undisputed letters of Paul (Galatians, 1 Thessalonians, 1 and 2 Corinthians, Romans, Philemon, and Philippians).
Phillip Vielhauer penned the classic study in the mid–twentieth
century making this allegation. He identified four areas in which
he believed the Paul of Acts was fundamentally incompatible
with the Paul of the epistles. (1) In Acts, Paul is positive toward
natural theology or general revelation (the idea that people can
come to some knowledge of God and even salvation through
looking at the design in creation—see especially his "Mars Hill"
speech in Athens [Acts 17:16–33]); in the letters Paul remains entirely negative (see esp. Rom. 1:18–32). (2) In Acts, Paul can still
treat the Law positively, as when he cuts his hair as part of a Jewish vow (18:18) or when he circumcises Timothy (Acts 16:3); in the
letters Paul stresses that the Law merely points out one's inability
to keep it, while the Jewish rituals and ceremonies belong to a
now-past age (see esp. Galatians 3–4). (3) In Acts, the resurrected
Jesus forms the centerpiece of the gospel message in virtually
every sermon recorded; in the letters, Paul focuses solely on the
crucifixion (1 Cor. 2:2). (4) In Acts, the hope of Christ's imminent
return has receded; in the letters it remains vibrant (see esp.
1 Thess. 4:15).[55]

None of these four alleged contradictions, however, fairly summarizes the complex data in either Acts or the epistles. Nothing in Acts suggests someone can actually be saved apart from Christ; even 17:27 speaks merely of people "finding" God in some unspecified sense, and even then Luke employs the unusual optative mood with the verb suggesting that Paul is doubtful that even this can be done. Romans 1:19–20, conversely, states very clearly that people should know that God exists based on creation. As for Paul's attitude to the Law, Acts can portray him as the great champion of grace alone (Acts 13:39), and the epistles can show Paul keeping the Law to try to win Jews to Christ (1 Cor. 9:20). The issue in both Acts and the epistles is whether a certain law is put forward as necessary for salvation. That Paul will resist to the hilt.

Turning to the question about the heart of the gospel, Acts 20:28 highlights Christ's blood atonement, while 1 Corinthians 15 teaches extensively on the resurrection. Clearly it is a matter of emphasis, not of contradiction, as to which writings stress the one aspect of Christ's work over against the other. Finally, Paul's epistles disclose that he recognizes he may *not* live to see Christ's return (e.g., Phil. 1:19–26), while Acts portrays Paul preaching that his day *is* the decisive turning point in the ages that will usher in God's judgment (Acts 17:31). David Wenham has ably surveyed these and related issues and concludes that the differences between Acts and Paul's letters are substantial enough to prove that *Paul* didn't write Acts! But the differences hardly demonstrate a fundamental tension between Paul and Luke. Each writer had his own reasons for emphasizing complementary portions of Paul's ministry.[56]

Hard Sayings and Missing Topics

In the previous major section of this chapter, I responded to numerous arguments *against* the reliability of the apparently historical portions of the New Testament. It is time now to turn to additional, positive evidence *for* its reliability. Two of these pieces of evidence form a natural pair. On the one hand, there are numerous "hard sayings" of Jesus in the Gospels that his first followers would not likely have invented. One example of a hard saying is that which

makes a very stringent demand on disciples, even when it seems
to contradict Jesus' own teaching elsewhere. For example, Luke
14:26 declares that Jesus told his would-be followers, "If anyone
comes to me and does not hate father and mother, wife and children, brothers and sisters—yes, even life itself—such a person
cannot be my disciple." Such a claim would have scandalized a
Jewish audience that took seriously the Mosaic commandment to
honor father and mother, a commandment which Jesus elsewhere
himself affirms (e.g., Mark 7:10). Fortunately for us, Matthew includes a parallel teaching of Jesus in a different context, explaining what he probably meant in Luke's setting as well: "Anyone
who loves their father or mother more than me is not worthy of
me; anyone who loves a son or daughter more than me is not worthy of me" (Matt. 10:37). Both Greek texts are of course translating
Jesus' original Aramaic, and in Semitic languages "love" and
"hate" often meant "choose" and "not choose" or "prefer" and
"not prefer."[57] Our love for God should so surpass our love for
family that the latter seems like hate in comparison. Now the saying is at least understandable, though still incredibly challenging.
But if either Luke or Matthew felt as free to tamper with the traditions he inherited as many scholars claim, it surely would have
been far easier simply to leave these kinds of sayings out.

In other instances, what makes a saying "hard" is that it appears to contradict the deity of Christ, which the early church so
quickly came to emphasize. For example, in Mark 6:5–6, Jesus'
power seems limited by the lack of faith in Nazareth: "He could
not do any miracles there, except lay his hands on a few sick people and heal them. He was amazed at their lack of faith." Or in
13:32, his knowledge seems limited: "But about that day or hour
[of Christ's return] no one knows, not even the angels in heaven,
nor the Son, but only the Father." Christian theology eventually
came to grips with such texts and spoke of Jesus not drawing on
his divine attributes (such as omnipotence and omniscience) except when it was his Father's will. But it would have been far easier for Mark simply to omit these sayings, in light of the confusion
they could potentially create. Something, however, kept him from
excluding them. Apparently these were "fixed points" in the tradition (see above, p. 35) that could not be eliminated if the narratives in which they appeared were to be recounted at all.[58]

A reverse phenomenon also supports the substantial historicity of the Gospels. Various early-church controversies described in Acts and the epistles never appear on the pages of the four Gospels. If the first Christians felt free to attribute to the historical Jesus teaching they believed the risen Lord was revealing to them, why do no teachings of Jesus ever address these particular controversies? We know from Acts 15 and Galatians 2 that the issue of circumcision, as part of the Judaizers' agenda to get Gentiles who were becoming Christians to obey all of the Jewish Law, threatened to tear the early church in two. The simplest way to have solved the controversy would have been for one of the participants in the Apostolic Council of Acts 15 to have cited Jesus' own teaching on the topic. We would then expect one of the Gospels to contain some teaching of Christ about whether or not circumcision would be required of his followers. But neither Acts nor the Gospels contain a single word attributed to Jesus to resolve that debate. Apparently the early church did *not* feel free to invent teachings of Jesus that it knew he did not proclaim during his earthly life. A similar example comes from 1 Corinthians 12–14. Speaking in tongues proved very divisive in Corinth. How better to solve the debate over speaking in tongues than to quote Christ somewhere? And surely we would expect to find a saying or two of Jesus on the topic in the Gospels. No such statement ever occurs! Indeed, a sizable list of contrasts can be compiled between issues that were significant for Jesus during his pre-crucifixion ministry in Israel and issues that proved important for the post-resurrection church. And the New Testament consistently keeps them separate.[59]

Moreover, on at least one occasion, when those concerns overlap, Paul clearly takes great pains to distinguish what Jesus said during his earthly life from what he believed Jesus was saying to him as he wrote his letters under divine inspiration. The example in question appears in 1 Corinthians on the topic of marriage and divorce. In 7:10–11, Paul proclaims, "To the married I give this command (not I, but the Lord): A wife must not separate from her husband. . . . And a husband must not divorce his wife." Here Paul summarizes the content of the teaching of the historical Jesus in passages like Mark 10:1–12 and parallels. But on the issue of an unbelieving spouse wanting to leave his or her partner after that person had become a Christian, Jesus had taught nothing. So Paul continues in 1 Corinthians 7:12, "To the rest I say this (I, not the Lord). If any brother has a wife who is not a believer and she is willing to live with him, he must not divorce her. And if a woman has a husband who is not a believer and he is willing to live with her, she must not divorce him." Paul is *not* claiming here that he is now no longer writing under inspiration! Verse 40 makes it clear that he thinks all his instructions in this chapter are Spirit-guided. Indeed, Paul here speaks with a tinge of irony since he is combating opponents in Corinth who claim that they alone have the Spirit. Instead, verse 12 means simply that he has to rely on what he believes God is telling him without being able to prove it by quoting a saying from the tradition of Jesus' earthly teachings. The same explanation doubtless accounts for verse 25. Far from casually mixing together the pre- and post-resurrection teachings of Christ, Paul carefully keeps the two separate. All this should increase our confidence in the historical trustworthiness of the Gospels.[60]

The Evidence of Non-Christian Writers

For some people, the only evidence that ultimately proves valuable is that of ancient writers who never became Christians. Even if one grants that Christians *could* write history without their biases unduly distorting it, there is always the possibility that they *did not* do this successfully. Of course, these same people seldom observe that non-Christians could be even more biased against Christianity and thus fail to present its historical origins fairly. We have proof that this happened frequently in the first millennium A.D. as the voluminous Jewish literature that formed the Mishnah, Talmuds, and various Midrashim increasingly censored and excluded references to Jesus (and other supposed apostates) as the centuries progressed. But it is nevertheless worth surveying what the oldest Jewish, Greek, and Roman literature does say about Jesus and other characters and events portrayed in the Gospels and Acts. Especially when we allow for these authors' biases, a remarkable amount of evidence does emerge that once again supports the historical reliability of the canonical documents.[61]

EVIDENCE FOR JESUS

By far the most extensive and interesting information comes from Josephus. Writing near the end of the first century, this Jewish historian produced a twenty-volume work called *Jewish Antiquities*—a history of the world from creation all the way to his own day! The surviving manuscripts contain two references to Jesus. In 20.197–203 we learn about the execution of James, the half-brother of Jesus, at the hands of the Sanhedrin in A.D. 62. Specifically, in section 200, Josephus refers to "James, the brother of Jesus who was called the Christ."[62] No serious scholars doubt the authenticity of this passing remark, so it alone demonstrates that Jesus existed.

The other passage in Josephus is considerably more detailed. It reads:

> About this time there lived Jesus, a wise man, if indeed one ought to call him a man. For he was one who wrought surprising feats and was a teacher of such people as accept the truth gladly. He won over many Jews and many of the Greeks. He was the Messiah. When Pilate, upon hearing him accused by men of the highest standing amongst us, had condemned him to be crucified, those who had in the first place come to love him did not give up their affection for him. On the third day he appeared to them restored to life, for the prophets of God had prophesied these and countless other marvellous things about him. And the tribe of the Christians, so called after him, has still to this day not disappeared. (18:63–64)

The problem with this passage is that Josephus indicates from the rest of his work that he remained Jewish throughout his life and did not embrace Christianity. So it remains highly unlikely that he would have actually written that Jesus was the Messiah, questioned his true humanity, or believed in his resurrection. Once we realize that it was Christians and not Jews who preserved the works of Josephus in the early centuries after his writing, it is natural to assume that some scribes "touched up" Josephus's work to make his testimony support Christian claims more explicitly. Moreover, a tenth-century Arabic work, Agapius's *Universal History*, refers to Josephus's testimony about Jesus, and its summary lacks precisely these three items, although it describes Josephus saying that Jesus' followers *reported* seeing him alive and that he was *perhaps* the Messiah. There is a growing scholarly consensus, therefore, that the passage in *Jewish Antiquities,* once rewritten at these three junctures, then closely approximates what Josephus actually penned.[63]

Later Jewish testimony, most of it found in the Talmud, is more tendentious in nature. In one text, Jesus is said to have been hanged on the eve of the Passover. Since Jews had already decided that crucifixion was comparable to hanging on a tree, this need not conflict with the Gospel accounts, particularly John's, which can be read as if Jesus were executed on the day before Passover (though recall our different interpretation above, p. 37). This same text, however, goes on to say that for forty days before the execution, a herald cried out, "He is going forth to be stoned because he has practiced sorcery and enticed Israel to apostasy." So it may be that the historical record here is somewhat garbled.

The charge that Jesus was a sorcerer, however, appears elsewhere in the rabbinic literature (see esp. *b. Sanh.* 107b), providing backhanded corroboration that Jesus did work miracles. Instead of denying that fact, Jewish writers simply attributed his power to the devil rather than to God. Interestingly, this approach emerges first on the pages of the Christian Gospels themselves (Matt. 12:24; Luke 11:15).[64] The same section of the Talmud that refers to Jesus' hanging also claims that Christ had disciples by the names of Mattha, Naqai, Nezer, Buni, and Todah. Four of these could be alternate or corrupt Hebrew spellings of Matthew, Nicodemus, John, and Thaddeus, while Nezer could refer to a Nazarene or follower of Jesus more generally.

Other explicit references to Jesus include a tradition in which a rebellious disciple is compared to one "who publicly burns his food like Jesus of Nazareth," a metaphor that refers to the distortion of Jewish teaching (*b. Sanh.* 103a). In several places, Jesus is called "Jesus ben (= son of) Pandera," and the second-century Christian writer Origen explains that the Jews believed that Jesus was the child of Mary by an adulterous relationship with a Roman soldier by that name (*Contra Celsum* 1:32). The name and hence the legend probably comes from a corruption of the Greek word *parthenos* for "virgin" and thus reflects garbled knowledge of the Christian tradition of the virginal conception. In still other texts, Jesus does not appear by name, but there is widespread agreement in Jewish tradition that he is in view. For example, the third-century Rabbi Abbahu declares, "If a man says to you, 'I am (a) God,' he is a liar; 'I am (a) Son of Man,' he will regret it; 'I go up to heaven,' he has said it but he will not be able to do it" (*p. Ta'an.* 65b). One can recognize echoes of the Gospel tradition in all three claims.[65]

Non-Christian Greco-Roman historians also make a half-dozen references to Jesus. Thallus (preserved only in the writings of the third-century historian Julius Africanus) referred to the darkness that occurred at the time of the crucifixion. Pliny the Younger, a Roman legate in the early second century, wrote to the emperor Trajan, requesting advice as to how to deal with Christians who refused to worship the emperor. In this correspondence he explained that Christians met regularly and sang hymns "to Christ as if to a god" (*Letters* 10.96.7). The early-second-century Roman historian Tacitus depicted Christians as those whose name came from "Christ who had been executed by sentence of the procurator Pontius Pilate in the reign of Tiberius" (*Annals* 15:44). At about the same time the Roman historian Suetonius referred to the expulsion of Jews from Rome during the reign of Claudius as due to a riot at the instigation of *Chrestus*. Most scholars believe this is a corrupt version of *Christus* (Christ) and that it was turmoil among Jews and Christians that Suetonius describes, mistakenly thinking Christ was personally present to instigate it. The reference "nevertheless points out Jesus as the leader of a band of dissident Jews, if not the founder of Christianity."[66] The late-first-century Greek writer Mara bar Serapion spoke of Jesus as the wise king of the Jews, while the Greek philosopher and historian Lucian of Samosata in his mid-second-century work, *The Death of Pergrinus*, referred to Christ's crucifixion (sec. 11) in a mocking treatment of the gullibility of Christians who revered their founder as a god. Finally, Origen recounted in some detail the charges of his pagan critic, Celsus, who recognized but disparaged "Jesus' ancestry, conception, birth, childhood, ministry, death, resurrection, and continuing influence."[67]

When one combines all this ancient non-Christian testimony to Jesus, there is more than enough to refute the persistent myth that lingers in certain circles that Jesus never existed![68] Modern readers may wonder why there was not a whole lot more preserved, to which two basic replies must be given. First, in these early years, no one yet knew that Christianity would one day become the dominant religion in the empire, much less throughout large portions of the world. Second, until well into the twentieth century, most history-writing has involved the exploits of kings and queens, military generals, the wealthy, office holders in religious institutions, and the like. A focus on the ordinary citizens of a particular country and on popular movements that did not interface with any political or ecclesiastical powers remained comparatively rare until the past century. We could argue that it is surprising that these non-Christian references to Jesus survived.

OTHER CHARACTERS AND EVENTS

When we turn to other characters in the Gospels and Acts, the situation proves quite different. Precisely because many of these are power brokers of various sorts, the non-Christian references become so abundant that we can present only a small selection of them here. Josephus alone provides a considerable amount of information about John the Baptist, Herod the Great, Antipas, Agrippa I and II, Annas, Caiaphas, and Pontius Pilate.[69] Josephus and the various Roman historians, of course, refer in detail to the different emperors who are also mentioned in the New Testament.

Borrowing heavily from the voluminous catalogue of information in Colin Hemer's magisterial work, we may itemize thirteen types of historical knowledge displayed in Acts that are corroborated by or at least fit in quite well with other historical sources.[70] In each case we give just one or two examples, though in most instances a large number exist.

1. *Common knowledge:* Luke recognizes that Augustus is the emperor's name (Luke 2:1) but correctly has a Roman official refer to him by his title (in Greek, *Sebastos*) in Acts 25:21 and 25. He also knows that corn-ship voyages sailed from Alexandria to Puteoli (28:11–13).
2. *Specialized knowledge:* Luke understands that Annas would still have been viewed as the high priest by Jews even after formally deposed by Rome (4:6). He is also aware of the details of the organization of a military guard—four squads of four soldiers each (12:4).

3. *Specific local knowledge:* Zeus and Hermes were popular gods in Lystra because of a legend that they had appeared there incognito centuries earlier. It is thus understandable that Barnabas and Paul should be mistaken for them (14:12). The voyage and shipwreck of Paul contains numerous items that could scarcely have been known unless someone had been on such a trip or was very familiar with the nautical technology of the day.[71]

4. *Correlations of date:* The information of Acts dovetails with other historical sources and enables us to provide dates for Herod Agrippa I's death, the famine in Judea, Claudius's expulsion of the Jews from Rome, Gallio's governorship in Corinth, and the change of procurators from Felix to Festus in Judea.

5. *Ability to fit the rest of Acts in with those dates:* Other indications of time in Acts create a harmonious fit with these details—Paul's one and one-half year stay in Corinth, nearly three years in Ephesus, and two years under arrest under Felix—enabling studies of the life of Paul to date with considerable precision (by ancient standards) each of Paul's missionary journeys and his stops along each route.[72]

6. *Details broadly suggestive of date:* The Synagogue of the Freedmen in Jerusalem was destroyed in A.D. 70; its accurate depiction in Acts 5:9 would have required knowledge of pre–70 conditions. Phrygia and Galatia were linked together for only a short time in the first century, exactly as Luke depicts them in 16:6.

7. *Correlations with Acts and the epistles:* Again there are an enormous number. Galatians 2:2 and 10 match elements of Paul's visit to Jerusalem also described in Acts 11:27–30. The superstition berated in Galatians 3:1 fits the Lystrans' mistake in identifying Paul and Barnabas with Greek gods, as already noted.

8. *Correlations within Acts:* The diverse nature of Paul's speeches perfectly matches what we know of the locations to which each is addressed, from skeptical, philosophical Athens at one extreme (17:16–34) to the Christian elders of Ephesus at the other (20:17–35).[73]

9. *Possible historical information preserved in textual variants:* While it is not likely to be what Luke originally wrote, the "Western" text of Acts 19:9–10 adds that Paul spoke each day in Tyrannus's lecture hall "from the fifth to the tenth hour" (i.e., from 11 A.M. to 4 P.M.—the hottest part of the day when the hall was most likely to be available), a probably accurate piece of information added by a later scribe.

10. *Unstudied allusions:* Tangential information, historically accurate, not likely to have been consciously fabricated, includes labeling the Antioch in Phrygia near the border of Pisidia as Pisidian Antioch (13:14), as others had done, to distinguish it from another Antioch located more centrally in Phrygia though never mentioned in Acts. Paul's accurate citation of Greek poetry, by Epimenides and Aratus, in Athens offers a second example (17:28).

11. *Differences of formulation within Acts:* Luke correctly uses the term "Hellenists" when speaking of Jews who have adopted Greek culture but calls people "Greek" when non-Jewish, non-Christian individuals are meant. Saul stops using his Jewish name, not at conversion, as careless Bible readers often mistakenly think, but when he begins ministry among the Gentiles (13:9).

12. *Particular selection of detail:* While not explicitly mentioned in other historical sources, inclusion of certain details of no obvious theological significance fits the genre of history-writing in a world that had not yet invented what we would call the historical novel.[74] One may compare the roles of Rhoda in 12:13–14 and Mnason in 21:16.

13. *Special idioms or cultural features:* Tertullus's ingratiating speech (24:2–4) perfectly matches the flattering oratory of Gentile lawyers speaking to Roman procurators. The governor's option to accept or refuse jurisdiction over a case from a separate province is likewise depicted unerringly in 23:34.

Any one of these specific items might not prove too much by itself, but the cumulative case for Luke's accuracy as a historian in

Acts becomes overwhelming when one discovers the sheer volume of such items that exist.

Archaeological Evidence

A particularly significant subcategory of corroborating external evidence outside of the Gospels and Acts, or any other explicitly Christian sources, is that which archaeology unearths. Once again, there are books filled with items that confirm the kinds of details in the New Testament that lend themselves to archaeological proof or disproof. In no instance has any detail been disproved; countless items have been corroborated. Again, we can just get our feet wet by dipping into some of the most famous or significant examples.[75]

THE FOUR GOSPELS

A remarkable amount of circumstantial detail in the Gospels receives support from excavations in Israel. Most of this serves to enhance our understanding of the historical, religious, and sociocultural background of Jesus' world. Thus one can see ruins of Herod's numerous building projects, the layout and function of the temple, the size and contents of a typical Palestinian home, the nature of Roman roads, and the like. Millstones, ritual immersion pools, and "Moses' seat" in a synagogue have all been unearthed, illuminating Gospel references to those items. In some cases, entire sites have been excavated—Capernaum's fourth-century synagogue, probably built on the foundations of the one from Jesus' day; Jacob's well at Sychar where Jesus met with the Samaritan woman; the pool of Bethesda with its five porticoes near the Sheep Gate in Jerusalem; the pool of Siloam, also in Jerusalem; and possibly the paving stones (Gabbatha or Lithostrotos—see John 19:13) outside Pilate's headquarters (assuming this to have been the Antonia Fortress).[76] The same is true for the location of whole cities. A first-century mosaic of a fishing boat with the inscription "Magdala" helped lead to the discovery of the location of the hometown of Mary Magdalene. Ruins of a Byzantine church east of the Sea of Galilee probably point to the location of Khersa (see above, p. 37), where Jesus exorcised the man with a legion of demons.

Some finds are quite recent. Not until 1961 was inscriptional (as opposed to literary) evidence unearthed at Caesarea Maritimis of Pilate as prefect of Judea during Tiberius's reign as emperor. In 1968 an ossuary (i.e., a bone box) of a crucified man named Johanan confirmed for the first time that Romans might drive nails through the feet or anklebones of executed victims. A first-century fishing boat was dredged up from the Sea of Galilee in 1986 after the worst drought in Israel in more than a century. Interestingly, it had room for exactly thirteen people, the amount of space that would have been required for Jesus and his twelve disciples all to fit in one vessel. The museum in which tourists may now view it has dubbed it "the Jesus boat," though of course we have no way of knowing if Jesus himself ever used it. In 1990, the tomb of what seems likely to be the high priest Caiaphas was discovered on Mount Zion in Jerusalem near the Old Testament site traditionally known as the City of David.[77] The most recent center of archaeological activity has been Bethsaida. Although to date no dramatic finds have emerged, many small artifacts, including numerous items relating to the fishing industry, have been dug up. But as this book goes to press, controversy swirls around another find, near Jerusalem—the possible ossuary of James, the brother of Jesus. The possibility that the inscription on the burial box, which reads "James," was carved by two separate hands, however, leaves scholars unsure as to which James was buried in it.[78]

Frequently, archaeology provides good "object lessons" for the interested Bible reader. In other words, sites that are not the actual locations of events from the Gospels nevertheless closely resemble what the real sites probably looked like. Thus, while the ornate Church of the Holy Sepulchre in Old Jerusalem is probably near the authentic site of the crucifixion and burial of Jesus, Gordon's Calvary—a skull-shaped outcropping of rock just above the modern-day Jerusalem city bus station—is so characteristic of the terrain that it probably looks something like the original site of Golgotha, explaining why that location was dubbed "the Place of the Skull." Or again, tourists are regularly shown a sizable plateau a few hundred feet up from the northwest shore of the Sea of Galilee and beneath the traditional "Mount of Beatitudes." Here the natural acoustics make it possible for someone standing partway up the hillside to be heard by large numbers of people at one time. This could be where Jesus preached his famous "Sermon on the Mount," but we simply have no way of telling because the Gospels do not give us enough information to determine a location.

Excavated artifacts can often give insights into specific words or customs. The single word *corban* ("dedicated to God") has been found on a Jewish sarcophagus as a warning to grave robbers. Glistening "whitewashed" tombs still dot the Kidron Valley and a portion of the slopes of the Mount of Olives, visually illustrating Jesus' metaphor in Matthew 23:27. Coins in abundance confirm the custom of minting Caesar's image on them, a point on which Jesus relied when he evaded the Jewish leaders' trick question about paying taxes.

Archaeology further holds the potential for illuminating the silences of the Gospels. Much excavation in the past twenty years has centered on Sepphoris, the original Herodian capital of Galilee before the construction of Tiberias in the 20s A.D. Interestingly, Sepphoris was only five miles from Nazareth and required a heavy infusion of construction workers during Jesus' youth and early adulthood. Is this where Jesus learned the Greek practice of "play-acting," from which the word *hupokritēs* ("hypocrite") is derived, a word not otherwise found in Hebrew or Aramaic, yet one Jesus used repeatedly against certain religious leaders (see esp. Matthew 23)? After all, a large, typically Greek-style theater has been dug up there. Does the Gospels' silence with respect to Sepphoris imply that when Jesus began his public ministry, he avoided this largely Gentile city because he understood his mission as "to the Jew first"?[79] Or does the fact that archaeologists have unearthed comparatively few pig bones even at Sepphoris—a characteristic of highly Jewish cities that kept kosher tables and avoided eating pork or ham—suggest that we have overestimated how Greek this city was?

One artifact of a quite different nature deserves brief comment. Small fragments of the Shroud of Turin, carefully guarded for centuries in Italy by Catholic authorities, were subject to a battery of scientific tests in 1988 at three different laboratories around the world. All the results independently concurred that this was an eleventh- or twelfth-century piece of cloth, much too recent to have been Jesus' burial shroud.[80] There is still no convincing explanation of the origin of the striking impression of a crucified

man imprinted on this cloth, but nothing is to be gained by arguing any longer for its authenticity.[81] Since many people around
the world have heard of this shroud, even though they know
nothing else about ancient biblical artifacts, this point is worth
emphasizing.

THE BOOK OF ACTS

When one turns to the archaeology of the plethora of sites mentioned in Acts, one scarcely knows where to begin, for so much
has been excavated. Leaving Israel means primarily following
Paul on his journeys (Acts 13–28).[82] In Pisidian Antioch, references to relatives of Sergius Paulus, the Cypriot ruler, were discovered, suggesting one reason why Paul and Barnabas headed
there after sailing from Cyprus to what today would be called the
Turkish mainland. Stone inscriptions enabled archaeologists to locate the sites of Lystra and Derbe, two other towns of southern
Galatia that Paul visited on his first missionary journey. Much of
ancient Ephesus has been reconstructed from ruins, including the
theater where the silversmiths rioted. An Ephesian statue of
Artemis, with what appear to be more than a dozen breasts attached to her chest, confirmed the worship of that goddess of fer-
tility and illustrates the kind of idolatry against which Paul
fought. In Thessalonica, inscriptional evidence for the first time
vindicated Luke's use of the otherwise unattested term
"politarch" to refer to the local, civil rulers (Acts 17:8—NIV "city
officials"). In Philippi, a possible site for Paul's brief imprisonment has been unearthed as well as the extensive *agora,* or market-
place, and a possible riverside location for the place of prayer
where Paul found Lydia and her companions.

Corinth, like Ephesus, contains many still-standing or re-
erected ruins. There the famous Gallio inscription enabled us to
confirm the existence and date of the local ruler before whom
Paul was tried. We can even see ruins of the *bēma* or "judgment
seat" where Gallio would have sat and presided over the trial.
The huge stone mountain called the Acrocorinth that towers in
the background still has ruins of the Roman fortress that later replaced the pagan temple atop it in the first century. There "sacred
priests" or "priestesses" engaged in sexual relations with "wor-
shipers" in order to achieve union with the gods. Little wonder

that sexual morality was a major preoccupation of Paul's in his first letter to the fledgling church there (see esp. 1 Corinthians 5–7). An inscription mentioning "Erastus" the "aedile" (a Latin word for a municipal official) corresponds strikingly to Paul's greetings from Erastus, "the city's director of public works," in Romans 16:23, written from Corinth. Athens, of course, contains the spectacular Parthenon but also Mars Hill, where Paul spoke to the Areopagus, and a lavishly rebuilt, modernized stoa—a pillared, covered walkway onto which shops surrounding the *agora* opened up.[83]

The Churches of Revelation

One does not normally think of the Book of Revelation as a document of a historical genre. But chapters 2 and 3, containing John's letters to the seven churches of Asia Minor, include numerous references that are illuminated by historical, and, more specifically, archaeological study.[84] The promise to Christian "overcomers" of "the tree of life" (Rev. 2:7) stands in stark contrast to the Artemis cult's tree shrine in Ephesus and the asylum it claimed to offer. The offer of a garland to Smyrna (v. 10) was appropriate for a city that had this as its well-known emblem of beauty. Pergamum was a center of Zeus worship, Asclepian healings, and the imperial cult, any or all of which are good candidates for "Satan's throne" (v. 13). Thyatira was the home of merchant guilds, including one for potters, that participated in idolatrous pagan ceremonies. Compare the smashing of pottery in verse 27.

But the most significant archaeological insights involve the seventh city, Laodicea. Laodicea was famous for its wealth (it rebuilt itself without Roman aid after an earthquake in A.D. 60), its black-wool industry, and a medical school that produced eye salve. By way of contrast to each of these three items, 3:18 declares the Christians there to be "wretched, pitiful, poor, blind and naked." Jesus knocks at this church's door to try to reclaim them for a more vibrant faith (v. 20). This gentle approach contrasts with the forced entry of Roman officials requiring lodging in this wealthy town, coming through an impressive triple gate in the city walls. Most significant of all, Laodicea did not have its own fresh water supply, so it had to be piped in either from the clear, cold mountain streams near Colossae or from the therapeutic hot springs near Hierapolis. Either way, by the time the aqueducts reached Laodicea, the water had become lukewarm. Thus, when Jesus says through John that he wishes the Laodiceans were either hot or cold (v. 15), *both* expressions are *positive* metaphors. This fact has been known since at least the work of Rudwick and Green a half-century ago, so preachers who perpetuate the myth that "cold" here means actively opposed to God unnecessarily mislead many![85]

A catalog of so much archaeological support for the basic historicity of the New Testament should not give the impression that there are no unsolved problems concerning the reliability of these documents. For example, there are at least two, and perhaps even three, plausible locations for the site of Emmaus. The problem of the date of Quirinius's rule in Syria (Luke 2:1), documented outside the Bible no earlier than A.D. 6, may have been solved by micrographic lettering on coins indicating that he held an earlier political position of power as well, but the marks are too small and uncertain for us to be sure.[86] (There are similar problems when one attempts to date the Theudas referred to in Acts 5:36; Josephus would appear to place his rebellion at a later date.[87] Literary sources thus contain the same prospects and pitfalls as archaeological sources.) But the overwhelming majority of archaeological discoveries have consistently pointed in the direction of upholding the trustworthiness of those portions of the New Testament documents with which comparisons may be made.

Other Early-Christian Evidence

The previous two main sections have focused on evidence, literary and archaeological, that could not have been tainted by Christian "bias." But the argument that *Christian* evidence must be "thrown out of court" is fallacious, as we have already seen (pp. 32–33). There is one final body of testimony, therefore, that dare not be neglected, which involves other Christian writings outside the Gospels and Acts. We survey this material in reverse chronological order, building from the least to the most significant.

By the early third century, if not already in the late second century, virtually all Christian narration of the public ministry of

Jesus and the first generation of church history relied exclusively on the material in the canonical Gospels and Acts. Even the apocryphal literature, for the most part, did not overlap with the canonical material but sought (even if fictitiously) to fill in the "hidden years" of Jesus' life, to disclose his supposedly secret teachings to certain followers after the resurrection, or to describe much later exploits of the apostles. As late as the mid–second century, however, the oral tradition of the foundational events of the church continued to circulate alongside the written New Testament documents. Papias, bishop of Hierapolis early in the second century, claimed that he trusted the oral tradition delivered to him by the successors of Christ's apostles more than any written texts (Eusebius, *Eccl. Hist.* 3.39.3–4).[88]

THE APOSTOLIC FATHERS

The collection of the earliest post–New Testament, orthodox Christian writings is known as the Apostolic Fathers. Primarily written during the first two-thirds of the second century, these documents include two epistles of Clement, bishop of Rome; a group of short letters by Ignatius, a famous Christian martyr; an epistle of Polycarp, a disciple of the apostle John; the *Didache*, or "Teaching" of the Apostles, an early handbook on practical matters in Christian ethics and church order; a harsh epistle against Judaism falsely ascribed to Barnabas; and a collection of visions, commands, and parables of Christian doctrines ascribed to the "Shepherd of Hermas."[89] Frequently, these works cite traditions found in the New Testament but with slightly different wording, so that we cannot be sure they are depending on the *written* forms of those traditions. In a handful of instances they cite teachings or events not found in the New Testament. Both of these features reinforce Papias's comment, suggesting that independent, *oral* testimony continued to circulate even after the Gospels and Acts were written. Because the Apostolic Fathers refer to a far larger number of details from the life of Christ and the earliest church than do non-Christian authors, to whatever extent that they provide independent testimony, a much larger percentage of information about Christian origins is confirmed than can be corroborated by our previous lines of argument. These references include much of Jesus' teaching in the Sermon on the Mount, a significant percentage of other teachings unique to the Gospel of Matthew, as well as Jesus' ethical exhortation more generally, clearly the most common part of the Gospels and Acts to be cited in early noncanonical Christian writings.[90]

REVELATION

Moving back to the end of the first century brings us to the last New Testament document, the Book of Revelation. Greg Beale believes he has identified numerous places where John, in putting together this Apocalypse, has drawn on the same independent traditions employing the Old Testament prophecies of Daniel that lie behind the Synoptic Gospels. The use of the Son of Man imagery, taken from Daniel 7:13–14, distinctive to both the Gospels and Revelation, is his most prominent example.[91] Louis Vos goes further, believing he has identified twenty-five passages in Revelation that demonstrate independent knowledge of traditions incorporated into the Synoptic Gospels,[92] but many of these are too allusive for us to be sure.

1 PETER

First Peter is dated by liberal scholars to the last decades of the first century, often to around the 80s. Conservatives, who believe Peter himself wrote the letter, ascribe it to no later than the mid-60s, since Peter was martyred under Nero in Rome between A.D. 64 and 68. This letter contains numerous apparent allusions to the Gospel tradition in different enough forms that direct literary dependence cannot be confidently demonstrated. Particularly telling are allusions to sayings in the Gospel of John, which, if John was authored in the 90s, could not have existed yet in written form even at the later date for 1 Peter. Three commonly cited examples are the statements about being born again in 1 Peter 1:2 (cf. John 3:3); loving Jesus without having seen him in 1:8 (cf. John 20:29); and being called out of darkness into light in 2:9 (cf. John 8:12).[93]

JAMES

The Epistle of James may in fact be the earliest of all the New Testament documents, written in the late 40s. But the evidence is ambiguous. James, the Lord's brother, could have written it as late as the early 60s, since he lived until A.D. 62. Those who ascribe the letter to another author at times place it into the 70s or 80s. But almost everyone believes that James is earlier than 1 Peter, just as 1 Peter was earlier than Revelation. Of all the New Testament epistles, none contains as many passages that verbally resemble the teaching of Jesus as does James. While there are no unequivocal quotations, there are about three dozen allusions, especially to the Sermon on the Mount/Plain in Matthew 5–7 and Luke 6:20–49.[94]

One needs to look no further than the first main paragraph of James's epistle to observe a pattern of allusions that remains consistent throughout the letter. "Consider it pure joy, my brothers and sisters, whenever you face trials of many kinds" (1:2; cf. Matt. 5:11–12—"Blessed are you when people insult you. . . . Rejoice and be glad"—and Luke 6:23); "that you may be mature and complete" (1:4; cf. Matt. 5:48—"Be perfect [or mature] therefore, as your heavenly father is perfect"); "you should ask God, who gives generously . . . and it will be given to you" (1:5; cf. Matt. 7:7—"Ask and it will be given to you"—and Luke 11:9); "but when you ask, you must believe and not doubt" (1:6; cf. Matt. 21:21—"if you have faith and do not doubt"—and Mark 11:23). These allusions involve all three of Matthew's main sources—Mark, Q, and M (uniquely Matthean material)—showing that James's knowledge of the Gospel tradition was widespread. But even if the letter was written as late as 60 or 61, it is unlikely that James had access to the completed Gospel of Matthew. He must have known Matthew's sources or the oral traditions behind them. The evidence begins to mount that the Gospels were based on tradition faithfully passed along, not invented by the Evangelists out of whole cloth.

PAUL

Finally, we come to the major epistles of Paul. Commentators across the theological spectrum all agree that Romans, 1 Corinthians, and 1 Thessalonians were written in the 50s, too early to have relied on any written Gospel. Yet there are a dozen or so clear quotations or allusions to teachings of Jesus that the Synoptics would later record. Romans 12:14 gives the command to "Bless those who persecute you; bless and do not curse" (cf. Luke 6:27b–28a par.); 12:17, to "not repay anyone evil for evil" (cf. Matt. 5:39);

and 13:7, to "give to everyone what you owe: If you owe taxes, pay taxes; if revenue, then revenue . . ." (cf. Mark 12:17 par.). In 13:8–9, Paul sums up the whole of the Law in the commandment to love one's neighbor (likewise Gal. 5:14; cf. Mark 12:31 par.); in 14:10 he condemns judging one's brother since we will all be judged (cf. Matt. 7:1–2a par.); and in 14:14 he declares, "I am convinced, being fully persuaded in the Lord Jesus, that nothing is unclean in itself" (cf. Luke 11:41; Mark 7:19b).

Three of the most explicit citations of Jesus by Paul occur in 1 Corinthians. In 1 Corinthians 7:10–11, Paul supports his views on marriage and divorce by giving the command, "(not I but the Lord): A wife must not separate from her husband. But if she does, she must remain unmarried or else be reconciled to her husband. And a husband must not divorce his wife." By stressing that this comes from the Lord, he does not mean to say that the rest of his teaching is uninspired, but that on this specific issue he can refer back to a teaching of the earthly Jesus.[95] In 1 Corinthians 9:14, Paul writes, "In the same way, the Lord has commanded that those who preach the gospel should receive their living from the gospel." Here he is referring back to the teaching that would later be recorded in Luke 10:7 ("workers deserve their wages"; cf. Matt. 10:10). The third quotation of a Synoptic-like passage is clearest of all. In trying to correct the Corinthian abuses of the Lord's Supper, Paul quotes extensively from the tradition of Jesus' words at his Last Supper, particularly parallel to the form Luke would inscribe (cf. Luke 22:19–20 par.). Because of their subsequent liturgical use, these have become known as the "words of institution" (of the Eucharist):

> For I received from the Lord what I also passed on to you: The Lord Jesus, on the night he was betrayed, took bread, and when he had given thanks, he broke it and said, "This is my body, which is for you; do this in remembrance of me." In the same way, after supper he took the cup, saying, "This cup is the new covenant in my blood; do this, whenever you drink it, in remembrance of me." (1 Cor. 11:23–25)

The verbs "received" and "passed on" in this kind of context are technical terms for the faithful transmission of oral tradition, as rabbis practiced with Torah.[96] Paul probably learned this information early in his Christian life as part of the elementary Christian "catechism" of the day. But this suggests that detailed knowledge of the actual wording of traditions that would a generation later be written up in the Gospels existed already in the 30s, since Paul's conversion dates to within two to three years of Christ's crucifixion!

In 1 Thessalonians 2:14–16, Paul compares the persecution the Thessalonian Christians endured to that of the Judean Christians at the hands of their countrymen who put Christ to death. These verses contain numerous allusions to parts of Matthew 23:29–38. In 4:15–5:4, even clearer parallels emerge. Paul introduces his description of the return of Christ in 4:15–17 as "according to the Lord's word," and most of the details of these three verses are paralleled in Jesus' "Olivet Discourse" (Mark 13 par.), in which the Lord described the events that would surround his second coming. In 5:2–4, the double reference to the day of the Lord coming like a thief in the night almost certainly harks back to Jesus' parable of the thief (Matt. 24:43; Luke 12:39), since so arresting a metaphor appears nowhere else in earlier sources. Numerous other texts, at times with slightly vaguer allusions, could be listed. But the point is clear—a significant, detailed, fixed body of oral tradition of Jesus' teaching circulated from the earliest days of the Christian church. The Gospel writers, in turn, relied on this tradition, not fanciful invention, in compiling his teaching.

The same proves equally true for details about the life and deeds of Christ. A summary of the most important pieces of biographical information that can be pieced together from the undisputed Pauline epistles would include his descent from Abraham and David, his upbringing in the Jewish Law, his gathering together disciples, including Peter and John, and his having a brother named James. We also learn about Jesus' impeccable character and exemplary life, his Last Supper and betrayal, and numerous details surrounding his death and resurrection.[97]

Early Christian Creeds

Oldest of all are passages used by Paul and Peter in their letters that scholars have identified as most likely predating the epistles in which they appear. Numerous texts of highly poetic Greek, filled with tightly packed formulations of fundamental Christian doctrine, in styles that often differ from those of the epistle writers themselves, and which seem to be set apart as self-contained entities within the letters in which they appear, prove likely candidates for early Christian creeds or confessions of faith. The clearest and most commonly cited examples are Philippians 2:6–11, Colossians 1:15–20, and 1 Peter 3:18–22.[98] These letters were most likely written in the early 60s, so that established creeds incorporated into them probably stem from no later than the 50s. But these (and other) confessions also show signs of early *Jewish* Christianity that flourished the most in the 30s and 40s, so they could be older still.

Yet it is precisely in this very early material that we often find some of the most exalted language about Jesus. He was "in very nature God" (Phil. 2:6), "the image of the invisible God" (Col. 1:15), and "has gone into heaven and is at God's right hand—with angels, authorities and powers in submission to him" (1 Peter 3:22). Such beliefs thus emerged early in the history of the church, not at some advanced stage of the "evolution" of Christian doctrine.[99] These passages also lend credibility to the exalted claims by and about Jesus on the pages of the Gospels themselves.

The most significant and astonishing pre-Pauline passage of all is 1 Corinthians 15:3–7. Once again Paul uses the technical language of the reception and delivery of Jewish oral tradition: "for what I received I passed on to you as of first importance." Here we come to the very heart of early Christian belief about Jesus—

> that Christ died for our sins according to the Scriptures, that he was buried, that he was raised on the third day according to the Scriptures, and that he appeared to Cephas [Peter], and then to the Twelve. After that, he appeared to more than five hundred of the brothers and sisters at the same time, most of whom are still living, though some have fallen asleep. Then he appeared to James, then to all of the apostles. . . .

The core of this catechetical information must have been taught to Paul very soon after he became a Christian. Dramatic corroboration of this comes from a leading German scholar who moved down a path from liberal Christianity to atheism during the 1990s. Writing extensively on the subject of the resurrection, Gerd Lüdemann argued that within the first two years of the Christian movement, Jesus' followers were confidently proclaiming his bodily resurrection from the dead. While Lüdemann does not believe that a genuinely supernatural event happened, he recognizes that the most responsible statement a historian can make is that the first Christians almost immediately believed that such a thing did occur.[100] It will not do to pretend that the story of the resurrection was a much later, mythological fabrication, long after the people who knew what really did or didn't happen were gone!

Miracles

The only thing that stops Lüdemann from moving from the observation that the first Christians *believed* Christ to be raised from the dead to the conviction that he *was* bodily resurrected is his candid presupposition that such things, or any truly miraculous events, can never occur. While the issue of the miraculous might seem better left for another book, I cannot altogether avoid it in this chapter, even though my remarks must be brief.[101]

SKEPTICISM AND RESPONSE

There are three major reasons many modern scholars believe miracles cannot happen. First, some believe science has disproved miracles. The most famous articulation of this conviction comes from the prolific German New Testament scholar and theologian of a half-century ago, Rudolf Bultmann, when he pontificated that "man's knowledge and mastery of the world have advanced to such an extent through science and technology that it is no longer possible for anyone seriously to hold the New Testament view of the world."[102] Ancient people simply did not have the understanding of the universal laws of cause and effect that we do and therefore believed in things that we cannot.

Second, others allow for the possibility of the miraculous in theory but insist that in practice there will always be a higher probability that a naturalistic explanation accounts for the mysterious. The classic exposition of this view came from the eighteenth-century Scottish philosopher David Hume, who defended his assertion by stressing how often the testimony of otherwise reliable witnesses can be mistaken, how often gullible people fall prey to mistaken interpretations of events, and how others are simply looking for miracles and thus are unable to analyze causes of unusual events objectively. Hume adopted a philosophical uniformitarianism, that is, stating that a person cannot attribute a cause to an event that he or she has not directly observed or experienced (or learned about from someone else who has).[103]

Finally, a third argument appeals to the apparent parallels in ancient religion and mythology. Similar stories were told about the Greek and Roman gods and goddesses. Near-contemporaries of Jesus, for example Apollonius in the Greek world and Hanina ben Dosa or Honi the Rain-maker in the Jewish world, are said to have worked miracles, some of them strikingly similar to the early Christian signs and wonders. We have therefore misread the literary genre of the biblical miracle stories, which were never intended to record sober fact but are fictitious accounts designed to teach theological lessons. Classically articulated in the mid–nineteenth century by David Strauss, this is today the dominant explanation for the miracle stories in the Bible among the most skeptical branch of scholarship.[104] Each of these three arguments merits a response.

In reply to the scientific claim, it is important to stress that in a post-Einstein, post-Heisenberg age, philosophers of science are increasingly less dogmatic about what can and cannot happen, recognizing that science by definition is the study of the repeatable and therefore cannot pass judgment on the existence of God.[105] If God, by definition a supernatural being who created the universe, does exist, then we must allow for the possibility of his occasionally interrupting the normal scientific laws of cause and effect to create what we call a miracle. Interestingly, even in this highly technological, scientific age, the substantial majority of American adults still believe in miracles, not least because dramatic answers to prayer and instantaneous, unexplained physical healings continue to happen too frequently to be denied.[106] Conversely, we must remember that already in the New Testament period, people knew that the dead did not normally rise and that the sick did not normally become whole instantly. Too often, we pontificate on the gullibility of primitive people in ways that simply are not true to history.

Even though it still finds supporters, the philosophical objection was refuted more than three centuries ago. The testimony of credible witnesses must still be taken into account, even if what they describe seems incredible. Some people are gullible, but not all are, and not all to the same extent. Some people most assuredly are looking for miracles and may believe they have found them through some process of "wish-fulfillment." But hardened skeptics have also been converted to Christian faith because of miracles they were most decidedly not looking for. And uniformitarianism proves too much; by its criteria, no person living in the tropics, in an age before global communication and modern technology, would have any reason to believe in ice! What is more, uniformitarianism masks an anthropological determinism; that is, it leaves no room for free human agency to create a new cause for an event never previously imagined.[107]

As for parallels in other ancient religions, it is not likely that they are responsible for generating the miracle stories in the Gospels and Acts. The classic Greco-Roman myths were about gods and goddesses who never lived true, human lives on earth. On those rare occasions when miracles were attributed to deified human heroes, like Asclepius (though even then there is debate if such a man ever existed), they were still people from centuries past whose portraits grew into detailed legends only after hundreds of years. Miracles that occurred in New Testament times at shrines dedicated to Asclepius probably can be accounted for by what today would be called psychosomatic processes.[108] Apollonius of Tyana lived after the time of Christ and the composition of the Gospels and Acts, so his supposed healings and resurrections cannot have influenced the first Christian accounts. Hanina has healing miracles attributed to him, but only via prayer, whereas Christ and the apostles commanded people to be healed directly, and they were. The only miracle attributed to Honi, as his nickname suggests, was rainmaking, a kind of miracle that is never portrayed in the Gospels and Acts. But, given the Christian belief that God worked through faithful Jews and that Satan can work counterfeit miracles, there is no reason necessarily to reject all ancient stories of other seemingly supernatural events.[109]

Positive Evidence

Not only do the standard objections to accepting the New Testament miracle stories fail to convince, additional positive evidence supports their historicity. We have already noted that both rabbinic tradition and Josephus conceded that Jesus worked miracles (pp. 47–48). Miracle stories are found in every Gospel and every supposed Gospel source, as well as in Acts, and references to Jesus and the apostles working miracles are scattered throughout the epistles as well (e.g., Rom. 15:19; 2 Cor. 12:12; Gal. 3:5; Heb. 2:4). Globally, the miracle stories amply satisfy even the old dissimilarity criterion, not to mention the criterion of double similarity and dissimilarity (see above, pp. 20–21). There are *partial* parallels in earlier Jewish and later Christian sources, but the heart of the distinctiveness of the biblical accounts is the directness and effectiveness of the miracles and their function as pointers to the decisive arrival of the kingdom of God. The miracles thus also satisfy the criterion of coherence with teaching of Jesus known to be both authentic and central. John Meier, in the most exhaustive scholarly investigation in modern times of the historicity of the Gospel miracle accounts, while stressing that not every account satisfies all the criteria, nevertheless concludes:

> The curious upshot of our investigation is that, viewed globally, the tradition of Jesus' miracles is more firmly supported by the criteria of historicity than are a number of other well-known and often readily accepted traditions about his life and ministry (e.g., his status as a carpenter, his use of *"abba"* in prayer, his own prayer in Gethsemane before his arrest). Put dramatically but with not too much exaggeration: if the miracle tradition from Jesus' public ministry were to be rejected *in toto* as unhistorical, so should every other Gospel tradition about him.[110]

That is not of course Meier's conclusion; instead, there is strong reason to believe, even on purely historical grounds, in the substantial reliability of the miracle tradition.

RESURRECTION

Again, brief remarks seem wholly inadequate, but excellent books pursue the topic further,[111] most notably N. T. Wright's recent, magisterial *The Resurrection of the Son of God*.[112] No compelling alternative explanation has yet been proposed to account for the resurrection belief of the first Christians. The ideas proposed in older, popular literature that Jesus never really died on the cross, that his disciples stole the body, that the women went to the wrong tomb, or that more than five hundred "witnesses" over a forty-day period in several different geographical locations all experienced the identical "mass hallucination," have all been rightly discarded by the vast majority of contemporary scholars. The most popular scholarly alternative today is that the resurrection is the product of a later mythologizing process of an original tradition that did not include a supernatural return from the dead. But the evidence of 1 Corinthians 15 alone is sufficient to disprove this, as we have seen (pp. 64–65). What is more, it is the kind of explanation that might make sense if Jesus had been a Greek who preached in Athens and if his followers a generation later had become predominantly Jewish. Greece, after all, for the most part, believed only in the immortality of the soul. Jews were comparatively unique within the first-century Mediterranean world in believing in a full-orbed bodily resurrection. But, of course, this is the reverse of the actual geographical progress of the gospel. If anything we should have expected an increasingly Hellenistic Christianity more and more to play down or to excise references to the resurrection of a body.[113]

Not only do the alternatives to Jesus' bodily resurrection fail to convince, but six additional arguments also provide strong evidence in favor of its historicity. We have already mentioned the early testimony of Paul. In addition to 1 Corinthians 15, there are more than a dozen other references to Christ's resurrection in the indisputably Pauline epistles written no later than the 50s (Rom. 4:24, 25; 6:4, 9; 8:11, 34; 10:9; 1 Cor. 6:14; 2 Cor. 4:14; 5:15; Gal. 1:1; 1 Thess. 1:10; etc.). Second, no other explanation adequately accounts for why the first *Jewish* Christians (i.e., not just Gentiles) altered their day of worship from Saturday to Sunday, especially when their Law made Saturday (Sabbath) worship one of the inviolable Ten Commandments (Exod. 20:8–11). Something objective, astonishingly significant, and datable to one particular Sunday morning must have generated the change. Third, in a culture in which women's testimony was often inadmissible in a law court, who would invent a foundational "myth" in which all the first witnesses to a hard-to-believe event were women? Fourth, the restrained accounts of the New Testament differ dramatically from the bizarre apocryphal descriptions of resurrection invented in the second century and beyond. Fifth, in the earliest centuries of

Christianity, no tomb was ever venerated, separating Christian response to the death of their founder from virtually all other religions in the history of humanity. Finally, what would have led the first Jewish Christians to reject the interpretation bequeathed to them from Deuteronomy 21:23 that a crucified messiah, by the very nature of his death, demonstrated that he was cursed by God? Once again, it is easier to believe an admittedly supernatural event than to try to explain away all these strange facts by any other logic.[114]

Conclusion

We have surveyed a vast terrain in this chapter, trying to offer brief introductions to each topic, with references to where each may be pursued in greater detail. Certain arguments and certain parts of the various lines of reasoning prove stronger than others. Cumulatively, however, an impressive case can be made for the general trustworthiness of the Gospels and Acts, via historical criteria alone. People who choose to believe more of the accounts than historical reasoning by itself can support do so by a "leap of faith," to be sure. But it is a leap in the same direction that the vast majority of the historical evidence is already pointing. And every historian of the ancient world regularly reaches provisional conclusions about the reliability or unreliability of a given source, which then color his or her attitude to those parts of that source that can neither be confirmed nor contradicted. Because the Gospels and Acts prove reliable in so many places where they can be tested, they should be given the benefit of the doubt in those places where they cannot.

CHAPTER 2

Was Paul the True Founder of Christianity?

In the mid–nineteenth century, the German New Testament scholar Ferdinand Christian Baur proposed a sweeping revision of the traditional understanding of Christian origins. Borrowing from the philosophy of history of G. W. F. Hegel, the same man who inspired Karl Marx in the political arena, Baur believed he saw a process of "thesis-antithesis-synthesis" in the earliest generations of church history. One branch of Christianity followed Peter, who remained relatively faithful to the Jewish teaching of Jesus. Paul, however, represented an opposing approach, influenced more by Greco-Roman culture. Later generations then created a synthesis of the two. At the end of the nineteenth century, another German liberal, William Wrede, built on the work of Baur and labeled Paul the second founder of Christianity.[1] Writers in other disciplines were even less muted in their descriptions. The famous English playwright George Bernard Shaw wrote about "the monstrous imposition on Jesus," while nihilistic philosopher Friedrich Nietzsche called Paul "the first Christian" and "the Jewish dysangelist" (i.e., a bearer of bad news rather than an "evangelist" or herald of good tidings).[2]

A superficial comparison between Jesus and Paul certainly does disclose differences more quickly than similarities. Paul seems to quote or allude to Jesus' teachings only rarely and to say even less about Christ's life. Paul focuses instead on the meaning of Jesus' death and resurrection and employs christological categories that make Jesus a very exalted, divine being. Particularly for people who do not find the Gospels terribly trustworthy, who doubt that Jesus ever acted like or claimed to be more than a prophet, Paul seems to operate in an altogether different world.

In the first half of the twentieth century Rudolf Bultmann worked as hard as anyone to keep Jesus and Paul distant from one another. But for Bultmann, faith did not depend on historical evidence but on the witness of God's Spirit to a person through his Word. One could affirm traditional Christian doctrine as a believer, by faith, even if one's studies as a historian led to radically different depictions of Christian beginnings. Bultmann also became famous for appealing to 2 Corinthians 5:16 ("So from now on we regard no one from a worldly point of view. Though we once regarded Christ in this way, we do so no longer") and claiming that this meant that, as unbelievers, the disciples thought it was important to evaluate the historical Jesus but that, as believers, they recognized that the earthly Jesus was unimportant. What mattered was to worship the risen Lord.[3]

In the second half of the twentieth century, the pendulum began to swing away from these positions of extreme skepticism. Commentators agreed that 2 Corinthians 5:16 was contrasting two different evaluations of Christ before and after his resurrection—one which did not view him as the divine Messiah and one which did.[4] Conservative scholars like F. F. Bruce and J. W. Fraser wrote important books highlighting the continuity between the lives and teachings of Jesus and Paul,[5] generating a growing confidence in the similarity between the two men even in less conservative circles.[6] In recent years, no one has done more to champion this cause than British evangelical David Wenham, in two important books and in several articles on the topic.[7]

But skepticism dies hard and old theories are resurrected in new garb. At the beginning of this new millennium, Michael Goulder, from the University of Birmingham, has modified and re-presented Baur's theory, at least with respect to the tension in Corinth, suggesting that Paul had to combat Petrine Christianity as part of what he considered to be false teaching.[8] And Gerd Lüdemann, whose views on the resurrection we discussed in the last chapter (pp. 64–65), goes even further than Wrede to call Paul the true founder of Christianity.[9] The idea that the move from Jesus' own teaching to Paul's theology of Jesus can be summed up with the title "from Jewish prophet to Gentile god"[10] continues to surface!

Paul's Knowledge of Jesus' Teachings

The obvious starting point in replying to these charges involves the same texts I presented briefly in the previous chapter, texts that demonstrate Paul's awareness of the teachings of Christ (pp. 61–63). There my purpose was merely to argue that the presence of quotations or allusions to Jesus' words in letters written before the composition of any written Gospel demonstrated that Christ's teachings were circulating by word of mouth and being relatively carefully preserved. Here we need to go into much more detail, looking at these and other texts to determine just how much of Jesus Paul knew and how carefully he used what he knew.

THE CLEAREST REFERENCES

A Liturgical Text

By far the most extensive direct quotation of Jesus in Paul's epistles appears in 1 Corinthians 11:23–25:

> For I received from the Lord what I also passed on to you: The Lord Jesus, on the night he was betrayed, took bread, and when he had given thanks, he broke it and said, "This is my body, which is for you; do this in remembrance of me." In the same way, after supper he took the cup, saying, "This cup is the new covenant in my blood; do this, whenever you drink it, in remembrance of me."

Here Paul appeals to technical Jewish terminology for the transmission of oral tradition with the verbs "received" and "passed on" (see above, p. 62). This is information that he would have been taught very early in his Christian life. Celebrating the Lord's Supper in memory of Jesus' Last Supper characterized the church's worship from its inception (see Acts 2:42). Paul's wording proves especially close to Luke's version of the Last Supper (Luke 22:19–20), even though all three Synoptic writers include reasonably similar accounts. Although Luke regularly modifies

Mark where the two share accounts of an episode in Christ's life, many scholars think Luke drew on a special source, especially for distinctive material relating to the last week of Christ's life, and that the version shared by Luke and Paul reflects the oldest existing account of the Last Supper.[11] Whether or not this is the case, Paul clearly came to believe in the substitutionary, atoning death of Jesus early on, based on the very claims Jesus himself made about his upcoming death. Paul certainly elaborates on the topic throughout his epistles far more than Jesus did, but the two are in fundamental agreement on the issue.

Ethical Teachings

A less direct or extensive reference to a teaching of Jesus appears in 1 Corinthians 9:14, in which Paul writes, "In the same way, the Lord has commanded that those who preach the gospel should receive their living from the gospel." Here Paul is referring to the teaching of Jesus preserved in Luke 10:7 and Matthew 10:10 that workers deserve their wages. Because of the more explicit financial context, Paul probably again is drawing on the Lukan form of a so-called Q-saying (material found in both Matthew and Luke but not in Mark), and it is the form of the saying usually deemed to be the oldest, most literal translation of Jesus' words. It is sometimes alleged that Paul feels free to disobey Christ's commands, since in Corinth he refuses to accept money for ministry. But Jesus' words enunciated a principle that what we would call "full-time Christian workers" deserve financial support from fellow Christians. He never said that people could not voluntarily relinquish their right to receive that support, for a good reason such as Paul thought he had.[12]

First Corinthians 7 involves an interesting interplay between words Paul attributes directly to "the Lord" and those he takes credit for himself. In verse 10, he declares, "To the married I give this command (not I, but the Lord): A wife must not separate from her husband." In verse 12, however, he writes, "To the rest I say this (I, not the Lord) . . . ," as he goes on to deal with the situation of a Christian person with an unbelieving spouse who wants to leave the marriage. Although at first glance it might look like Paul is claiming inspiration for his first statement and then merely giving his personal opinion in the second case, it is more likely that he means that he knows that the historical Jesus taught against divorce in general (see Mark 10:2–12 par.) but that Jesus did not make any specific pronouncement about mixed marriages. Paul makes a similar distinction in verse 25: "Now about virgins: I have no command from the Lord, but I give a judgment as one who by the Lord's mercy is trustworthy." Paul *does* believe the Lord has guided him in giving him a conviction on the topic, but he recognizes he cannot quote the earthly Jesus in the process. Finally, verse 40 concludes the chapter with another of Paul's "judgment calls"—about the personal happiness of a widow who remains single—to which he appends his conviction that he too has "the Spirit of God," probably a gentle dig at the elitist teachers in Corinth who thought that they alone were in touch with God's Spirit.[13] Once again, the form of Jesus' teaching that Paul refers to at the outset of his discussion reflects the oldest version among the Gospel accounts.[14] Interestingly, too, Paul's preference for the single life throughout this chapter probably reflects Jesus' countercultural teaching that God does give the gift of celibacy to some believers (Matt. 19:10–12). Like Jesus in Mark 10:7 and parallel, Paul also appeals to the Genesis account of marriage (as leaving father and mother, cleaving to spouse, and becoming one flesh) in a nearby context (1 Cor. 6:16) that suggests he knew in some detail Jesus' teaching on the topic.

A cluster of allusions to the teachings of Jesus appears in Romans 12–15.[15] Romans 12:14 clearly refers back to Jesus' teaching in the Sermon on the Mount/Plain with its command to bless those who persecute believers, concluding "bless and do not curse." The appearance of the verbs for both blessing and cursing in Luke's form of this teaching (Luke 6:28) shows that Paul is again closer in his wording to the version of Jesus' saying usually deemed to be the older, more literal rendering (contrast Matt. 5:44). Romans 12:17 ("do not repay anyone evil for evil") may be an allusion to a portion of the sermon found only in Matthew (5:38—"do not resist an evil person"). Verses 18–19 seem to allude to Jesus' command to love one's enemies, especially as found in Luke 6:27 and 36, again the earlier forms of the tradition.[16]

Romans 13:7, with its wording about giving to everyone what is owed them, including taxes and revenue, clearly harks back to Jesus' response to the question of paying taxes: "Give back to Cae-

sar what is Caesar's and to God what is God's." Even the ex-
tremely skeptical Jesus Seminar colors this text red in Mark's
Gospel (12:17), identifying it as a rare saying of Jesus preserved
intact in its original form.[17] Paul's plea to the Romans to stop passing judgment on each other with respect to morally neutral matters (Rom. 14:13) probably alludes to another core teaching from
the Sermon on the Mount/Plain on not judging lest one be judged
(Matt. 7:1; Luke 6:37). The very next verse (Rom. 14:14) even more
plainly reiterates Jesus' declaration that all foods are now inherently clean (Mark 7:18–19 par.), a claim which is clearest in its oldest, Markan form. Christ's declaration may also lie behind Paul's
command in 1 Corinthians 10:27 to "eat whatever is put before
you." Alternately, this text may allude to Luke 10:7 on eating
whatever people provided the disciples as they went out on their
missionary journeys. In the latter case, it is interesting that consecutive verses of the same sermon would have been cited in different Pauline texts (recall 1 Cor. 9:14 on Luke 10:8), suggesting that
Paul knew larger blocks of teaching than just individual sayings
of Jesus.[18] Finally, Romans 15:1–3 explicitly refers back to the
model of Christ in not pleasing himself, using language that may
also echo his sayings about servanthood (cf. Mark 10:45 par.).

Except for the very explicit, lengthy citation of Jesus' teaching
at the Lord's Supper, all of these references thus far considered
fall into a clear pattern. Paul alludes to Jesus' words rather than
directly quoting him. The texts all involve Jesus' ethical instruction. And repeated references to Jesus' extended discourses suggest that Paul knew more than individual teachings circulating in
total isolation from each other. He was at the very least aware of
clusters of teachings on similar topics, if not the entire messages
themselves.[19]

Eschatology

The major *theological* topic that recurs in Paul's allusions to the
teachings of Jesus is eschatology. First Thessalonians 2:15–16 compares the persecution the Thessalonians are experiencing to that
unleashed by Jewish leaders in Israel "who killed the Lord Jesus
and the prophets and also drove us out. They displease God and
are hostile to everyone in their effort to keep us from speaking to
the Gentiles so that they may be saved. In this way they always

heap up their sins to the limit. The wrath of God has come upon them at last." These harsh pronouncements remind us of Jesus' words to certain hypocritical leaders among the Pharisees and scribes in Matthew 23, especially verses 32–36. There Christ declares, "Fill up, then, the measure of the sin of your ancestors" (v. 32), he describes how they have condemned prophets from past eras and how they are going to crucify him (vv. 34–35), and he concludes that "this generation" will be responsible for all this sin (v. 36). Again, all of these allusions have parallels in Luke as well (11:48–51), so we are looking at traditions with very old roots.[20] While commentators debate whether Jesus' and Paul's words were fulfilled in the shift from old to new covenant begun at Christ's crucifixion (A.D. 30) or in the destruction of Jerusalem in A.D. 70 by the Romans (or in both), there remain striking parallels between the statements of the two speakers.

In 1 Thessalonians 4:15, Paul announces that "according to the Lord's word, we tell you that we who are still alive, who are left till the coming of the Lord, will certainly not precede those who have fallen asleep." In verses 16–17, he goes on to explain that the Lord himself will return with a loud command and trumpet blast, the dead in Christ will be raised first, and then believers who are still alive will join them to welcome Jesus "in the air." While some commentators think that this is information that Paul has received directly from the risen Christ, it seems more likely that he is again alluding to teachings of the earthly Jesus. It is hard to know how much of what he adds after verse 15 forms part of this "word of the Lord," but it is interesting to observe various parallels to Jesus' teaching in the Olivet Discourse (in Mark 13; Matthew 24–25; and Luke 21). Specifically, Mark 13:26 and parallels describe the return of Christ from heaven (as in 1 Thess. 4:16a), as he sends out his angels (cf. v. 16b). The parallel in Matthew adds a reference to a loud trumpet (Matt. 24:31; cf. 1 Thess. 4:16c), while both Matthew and Mark go on to speak of a gathering together of all of God's people (Matt. 24:31; Mark 13:27; cf. 1 Thess. 4:15, 17).[21]

That the "Lord's word" refers to Jesus' teaching in the Synoptic Apocalypse, as Mark 13 and parallels are often called, is reinforced by even clearer allusions in 1 Thessalonians 5. In both verses 2 and 4, Christ's coming is likened to the surprise arrival of a thief in the night. This is such an unusual and striking metaphor (especially since Christ was revered but thieves are considered evil) that Paul would not likely have invented it. When we see Jesus in his parable of the householder employing the identical metaphor for the identical reality (Matt. 24:43–44; Luke 12:39–40), it becomes virtually certain that Paul is alluding to this particular passage. The sudden arrival of the end, while people think that the world will continue normally (1 Thess. 5:3), matches Jesus' teaching in the immediately preceding section of the Olivet Discourse (Matt. 24:37–42). The metaphor of birth pangs in the same verse corresponds to Mark 13:8 and parallel. Being sober and wakeful as children of the daytime (1 Thess. 5:4–6) echoes the call to watchfulness in Mark 13:33 and the entire parable of the bridesmaids in Matthew 25:1–13 (cf. also the watchful servants in Luke 12:35–38, which may have originally formed part of the same discourse).[22] Second Thessalonians 2:3–6 offers several equivalents to the description of the desolating sacrilege in Mark 13:14–20 and parallels. Once again, Paul seems to have known an entire sermon of Jesus and refers to it on several different occasions.[23] And the parables and metaphors cited are among the passages in the Synoptics most widely held to be authentic, even by scholars skeptical of large parts of the Gospel tradition. The lines of continuity between Paul and the historical Jesus again outweigh the differences.

OTHER POSSIBLE ALLUSIONS IN PAUL TO THE TEACHINGS OF CHRIST

One can easily get carried away looking for allusions or echoes of Jesus' teaching. A single word or phrase is usually not enough to establish direct dependence, even though certain scholars have exercised considerable ingenuity in trying to extend the possible points of contact between Jesus and Paul many times over.[24] But the following list of probably intentional parallels, while perhaps including one or two more items than the evidence entirely warrants, seems to strike a reasonable balance between positing too few and too many additional allusions.[25]

First Corinthians 13:2, with its proverbial reference to faith that can move mountains, probably alludes to Jesus' promise in Mark 11:23–24 about the disciples being able to tell a mountain to be taken up and cast into the sea. Matthew's parallel adds an explicit reference to "faith" in the first part of this saying (Matt. 21:21);

both versions refer to belief in the second half. Matthew 17:20 describes a similar saying of Jesus with reference to faith as small as a grain of mustard seed.

First Corinthians 1–2, with its contrast between those people this world deems wise and those to whom God discloses himself, contains numerous echoes of Jesus' pronouncement in Matthew 11:25–27 and Luke 10:21–22 that God reveals his will, uniquely through his Son, not to those who are considered wise on earth but to "little children." Verbal parallels include the Greek words for wisdom, understanding, God's good pleasure, what no one knows, the contrast between wise and foolish, and the words for hidden, eyes, seeing, and hearing.[26]

In 1 Thessalonians 4:8, Paul exclaims, "Therefore, anyone who rejects this instruction does not reject a human being but God, the very God who gives you his Holy Spirit." This principle may well allude to Jesus' own teaching in Luke 10:16: "Whoever listens to you listens to me; whoever rejects you rejects me; but whoever rejects me rejects him who sent me." Interestingly, the allusion again reflects Jesus' missionary discourse, confirming our earlier suspicions about Paul's knowledge of whole blocks of tradition.[27]

Galatians 1:15–16 describes Paul's conversion as God desiring to reveal his Son "in" Paul, after which Paul did not immediately consult "flesh and blood"—that is, other human beings. Given that Paul is defending his apostolic calling as just as authoritative as Peter's, and that he will shortly describe how he had to oppose Peter directly in Antioch (2:11–14), it is tempting to suspect an allusion to Jesus' own response to Peter's confessing him as Messiah: "This was not revealed to [or "in"] you by flesh and blood, but by my Father in heaven" (Matt. 16:17). Although this portion of the episode is not found in Mark, there are numerous Semitisms in Matthew's additions that make it likely Jesus actually said these things.[28]

Readers of 1 Corinthians 5:1–5 often wonder how to fit Paul's commands for excommunicating the incestuous church member with Jesus' principles in Matthew 18:15–17. It is possible that the less drastic steps outlined in the first part of the latter passage had already been taken and not had their desired effect. At any rate, it is striking that Paul's commands to deliver the man over to Satan (v. 5)—at the very least referring to disfellowshiping—precisely mirror the extreme measures Jesus invokes, if all else fails, at the end of his instructions.

In Galatians 5:14, Paul explains that "the entire law is fulfilled in keeping this one command: 'Love your neighbor as yourself.' " This conclusion closely matches Jesus' own declaration that all the Law and the Prophets "hang on" the double love-command of the Old Testament (of God and neighbor) (Matt. 22:40). Both Jesus and Paul explicitly cite Leviticus 19:18 in these two contexts; it is not likely that each would have independently picked the identical text to form part of their summaries of the greatest commandment(s).

Colossians 1:5–6 describes "the true word of the gospel" as "bearing fruit and growing throughout the whole world." Although similar agricultural metaphors were common enough in ancient Judaism, one does think of Jesus' parable of the sower, which also likens the preaching of the word to a sower of seeds, some of which grow enough to bear fruit (Mark 4:3–9 par.). Given that a variety of other texts in Paul's letters seem to echo language from this parable and/or its interpretation (vv. 14–20 par.)—most notably 1 Thessalonians 1:6 and 2:13 on receiving the word with joy despite persecution and accepting the word that was heard—it is quite possible that Paul was familiar with the parable itself. Intriguingly, in Acts 17:18 some of the Athenian philosophers insult Paul's speech by calling him a *spermologos*—etymologically a "seed wordsmith." The term is a rare, vulgar Greek expression for a second-rate speaker, who merely repeats someone else's philosophy without really understanding it. One wonders why the culturally elite philosophers would stoop to use it unless it captured one of Paul's emphases particularly well—speaking about seeds. Might Paul have used the sower and other seed parables of Jesus widely in his teaching?[29]

Throughout Paul's letters, the contrast between "flesh" and "S/spirit" plays an important role (see, e.g., Gal. 5:16–17; Rom. 8:12–13; 1 Cor. 3:1–3). In the Greek language more generally, "flesh" normally does not have the Pauline sense of "fallen human nature." The contrast is not common in the Gospels either, but Jesus' words to his closest followers in the garden of Gethsemane afford a striking parallel: "the spirit is willing but the flesh is weak" (Mark 14:38 par.). It seems likely that Paul was familiar with the tradition of Jesus' significant pronouncement during his agonizing ordeal.

A number of texts in Paul refer to serving one another and often use Christ as the model of a servant (e.g., Rom. 15:1–4; 1 Cor. 10:33–11:1). Particularly noteworthy is the famous "hymn" in Philippians 2:5–11, in which Christ's gracious condescension to humanity in the incarnation is described as "taking the very nature of a servant" (v. 7). One suspects that Paul may be echoing Jesus' own declaration that "even the Son of Man did not come to be served, but to serve, and to give his life as a ransom for many" (Mark 10:45 par.).[30]

Second Corinthians 1:17 presents Paul describing his change in travel plans due not to his fickleness but to the changed situation in Corinth. Probably anticipating charges against him, he asks, "Or do I make my plans in a worldly manner so that in the same breath I say both 'Yes, yes' and 'No, no'?" This is a curious way of describing vacillation in planning, unless Paul and/or the Corinthians are echoing Jesus' commands about oath-taking in Matthew 5:37: "All you need to say is simply 'Yes,' or 'No'; anything beyond this comes from the evil one."

Several interesting observations emerge from this list of possible allusions. To begin with, most come from sayings of Jesus widely agreed to be authentic, so that Paul is demonstrating not merely awareness of the Gospel tradition but knowledge about the historical Jesus himself. Second, the vast majority come from the undisputed letters of Paul (the exception is Colossians, which many scholars nevertheless consider Pauline). Third, for Paul to allude to teachings of Jesus rather than citing them verbatim requires that his audiences are familiar with the tradition in some detail so that they will recognize the allusions.[31] Finally, given that most of the more directly quoted (as well as the more allusively cited) texts are not formally described as a word of the Lord, it is probable that other passages in Paul's letters also allude to sayings of Jesus not otherwise preserved in the Gospel tradition (compare the "red-letter" verse in Acts 20:35).[32]

Paul's Knowledge of Other Elements of the Gospel Tradition

Chapter 1 presented a skeletal list of the most secure features of Jesus' life, apart from explicit teachings, of which Paul demonstrates a knowledge (p. 63). Stanley Porter presents a somewhat comparable list of what Paul seems "to know about Jesus the man":

> he was born as a human (Rom. 9.5) to a woman and under the law, that is, as a Jew (Gal. 4.4), that he was descended from David's line (Rom. 1.3; 15.12); though he was not like Adam (Rom. 5.15), that he had brothers, including one named James (1 Cor. 9.5; Gal. 1.19), that he had a meal on the night he was betrayed (1 Cor. 11.23–25), that he was crucified and died on a cross (Phil. 2.8; 1 Cor. 1:23; 8.11; 15.3; Rom. 4.25; 5.6, 8; 1 Thess. 2.15; 4.14, etc.), was buried (1 Cor. 15.4), and was raised three days later (1 Cor. 15.4; Rom. 4:25; 8:34; 1 Thess. 4.14, etc.), and that afterwards he was seen by Peter, the disciples and others (1 Cor. 15.5–7).[33]

But we can probably extend this list as well.

"Born of a woman" in Galatians 4:4 is just odd enough, if all Paul wants to say is that Jesus was truly human, that perhaps he is alluding to the tradition about a *virginal* conception—born only of a woman and not also of a man.[34]

Paul's language about salvation in Jesus, "who rescues us from the coming wrath," may well betray knowledge of John the Baptist's teaching to the crowds about fleeing from the coming wrath of God (Matt. 3:7 par.).

That Paul believed in baptism as the initiation rite for Christians suggests he knew both John's baptism in general and Jesus' support for John in agreeing to be baptized by him (Mark 1:9–11 par.). But there may be an even more specific allusion to the Spirit's descent onto Jesus at his baptism when Galatians 4:6 proclaims that "God sent the Spirit of his Son into our hearts."[35]

Second Corinthians 5:21 affirms Christ's sinlessness, which requires considerable knowledge of the details of his life. This affirmation may also suggest that Paul knew the story of Jesus' successful resistance of the devil's temptations at the outset of his ministry, perhaps the greatest threat to that sinlessness at any point in Jesus' life (Matt. 4:1–11 par.).

In 1 Corinthians 1:22, Paul makes the generalization, "Jews demand signs and Greeks look for wisdom." The latter is evident from Paul's ministry throughout the Greco-Roman world, as disclosed both by Acts and the epistles. But nothing elsewhere in those books shows Jews demanding signs from Paul. In the Synoptic Gospels, however, certain Jewish leaders repeatedly ask Jesus to perform a miracle as an utterly convincing sign of his identity. Whenever Christ senses that such a request comes merely from a hardened heart that wants to taunt him, he refuses (Mark 8:11–13 par.; Matt. 12:38–39 par.; Luke 23:8–9; John 4:48). Probably Paul has these kinds of occasions in mind.[36]

Paul's concern for the poor, nowhere presented in more detail than in 2 Corinthians 8–9, clearly takes its cue from Christ's model: "For you know the grace of our Lord Jesus Christ, that though he was rich, yet for your sake he became poor, so that you through his poverty might become rich" (8:9). In context, this declaration need mean nothing more than that Christ gave up the incomparable glories and wealth of heaven for the drastic limitations of life on earth. But it could also reflect Paul's knowledge of the modest lifestyle that Christ adopted. At birth, his family was too poor to offer the standard animal sacrifices, so they were allowed to substitute birds instead (Luke 2:24; cf. Lev. 12:8). As a carpenter during his young-adult years, Jesus may have reached the level of what we would today call the lower middle-class.[37] But his voluntarily adopted itinerant ministry, dependent on the hospitality of others, means that he most likely reverted to a level closer to the poverty line at times (cf. esp. Luke 8:1–3; 9:57–58 par.). And Paul may well have known all this, especially since he seems to have come from a more well-to-do background and consciously imitated Christ in abandoning his resources for a hard life of itinerant ministry.[38]

In 2 Corinthians 3:18, Paul describes believers as "being transformed into his likeness with ever-increasing glory," using the same Greek verb that is found in the Gospel accounts for Jesus' transfiguration (Mark 9:2 par.). Given that the larger context of 3:1–4:6 explores the contrasting degrees of glory between the old and new covenants, parallel to the brilliance on Moses' face when he descended from Mount Sinai contrasted with the greater brilliance of Jesus, it is natural to suspect that Paul knew the story of Christ on the Mount of Transfiguration.[39] If he did, then an otherwise more speculative suggestion takes on a greater probability. The same original Hebrew or Aramaic may well underlie the Greek words usually translated "pillars" and "standing ones," making one wonder if the reason Paul says that the leading apostles in Jerusalem were reputed to be "pillars" (Gal. 2:9) was that three of them had been among those "standing" in Jesus' presence when he saw the kingdom of God come in power at the transfiguration, as Mark 9:1 and parallels predicted.[40]

I have already mentioned that Paul may have known Jesus' teaching about coming not to be served but to serve (p. 81). But he probably knew a number of details about Christ's life that fit a larger model of servant leadership, because of Paul's repeated teaching on the topic. Particularly interesting is 2 Corinthians 10:1, in which Paul refers to the "meekness and gentleness of Christ" (even if ironically), suggesting a knowledge of that characteristic demeanor of the Lord and perhaps even the beatitudes specifically commending a similar behavior among disciples.[41]

Numerous Pauline texts commend the imitation of Christ. Sometimes the command is given explicitly (1 Cor. 11:1; 1 Thess. 1:6); often it is more implicit (Phil. 1:21; 2 Cor. 3:18; Rom. 6:17; 8:15–16; 13:14; 15:1–6). Either way, this theme requires detailed knowledge of Jesus' behavior.[42]

Once again our list could be lengthened, but some items would be more speculative. Using only the undisputed epistles and referring to elements of the Gospels usually deemed to be largely authentic, I have compiled a significant list of items about Christ's life that Paul likely knew. The list probably reflects only a small minority of what Paul actually knew, since these data, like the allusions to Jesus' teaching, emerge only when issues in local churches warranted referring to them. It is inherently probable that one who so zealously persecuted the church and then had such an about-face after his Damascus Road experience would have wanted to learn a lot of historical information about Jesus of Nazareth.[43] Curiosity alone usually generates historical interest in people one so strongly opposes or serves.[44] The twin notions, that (1) there is little indication in Paul's epistles of knowledge about the historical Jesus and that (2) Paul would have had little interest in the topic, both prove highly improbable.

Reasons for the Remaining Silence

But even if my entire argument thus far proves convincing, it is natural to ask why there is not even more explicit reference back to Jesus' words and deeds. (The question in part resembles the question from chapter 1 about why there isn't more non-Christian treatment of Jesus.) From one point of view I can argue that it is surprising that there is as much as we *do* find, given Paul's lack of knowledge of Jesus during his earthly life, his independent personality and ministry, his changed context of mission in the Greco-Roman world, and so on. Nevertheless, there are a number of other points that can be made in reply to the question of "why not more?"[45]

First, we must remember that none of Paul's letters reflects his initial evangelism of the communities he addressed. Undoubtedly, as Paul and other first-generation Christian preachers introduced the gospel to people who had not previously heard it, they would have had to tell the story of Jesus in some detail. But none of the epistles reflects this stage of ministry; rather, they presuppose it and build on it. In short, Paul's audiences already know the basic story of Jesus' life, death, and resurrection. They wouldn't have become Christians otherwise! The sermons in Acts which *do* represent initial evangelistic preaching are drastically abbreviated summaries of what were clearly far more extensive messages. Even so, one may detect an outline of what must have included considerable information about the teachings and deeds of Christ. Acts 10:36–38 reflects this outline most clearly:

> You know the message God sent to the people of Israel, announcing the good news of peace through Jesus Christ, who is Lord of all. You know what has happened throughout the province of Judea, beginning in Galilee after the baptism that John preached—how God anointed Jesus of Nazareth with the Holy Spirit and power, and how he went around doing good and healing all who were under the power of the devil, because God was with him.

C. H. Dodd exaggerated only slightly when he suggested that this outline could have provided the framework for the narrative composed by the first Gospel writer, Mark.[46] C. F. D. Moule shows that a similar pattern can be traced more generally in several other sermons in Acts as well.[47]

Second, none of the rest of the New Testament epistles has any larger number or contains any clearer references to the life and teachings of Jesus, even in those letters written late enough to be aware of and to utilize the written Gospels. We saw in chapter 1 that James and 1 Peter each has a number of allusions, but they do not directly quote Christ either. Their dates, however, are disputed. The letters that conservative and liberal scholars alike normally date late enough to be aware of all four of the Gospels are the epistles of John. Whether the product of the apostle himself or of a "Johannine school" of his followers, they could certainly have been expected to refer back to Jesus' sayings and ministry as presented in the Fourth Gospel, similarly authored by John or his followers. But 1, 2, and 3 John contain *no* undisputed allusions at all; the only clearly possible allusion would involve Jesus' love command (compare 1 John 2:7–11 with John 15:9–17). Thus it would appear that epistles simply are not the place to expect to find large numbers of references to the details of the life of Christ.

Third, these first two points both suggest that epistles represent a literary genre that the first Christians did not think fit the dissemination of basic historical information about the earthly Jesus. They were not used for what we have come to call "catechetical instructions" of the foundations of one's faith. Corroboration for this conclusion comes from the epistolary literature of the first half of the second century. Again one finds a fair number of verbal allusions to sayings of Jesus and a handful of more direct quotations, but no greater proportion of references than in Paul's letters. This will change as one moves to the second half of the second century, by which time the Gospels are clearly treated as Scripture and cited more directly and more frequently, as one might have expected earlier epistles to do as well. But if the period from A.D. 100–150 does not yet disclose this pattern, we surely should not expect to see it in letters having already been composed by Paul in the 40s, 50s, and 60s of the first century.[48]

Fourth, first-generation Christianity quickly recognized that the most important things about Jesus' life were his death and resurrection. His ethical teachings and mighty miracles ultimately would have proved irrelevant were he not who he said he was, a divine Messiah coming to atone for the sins of the world and to conquer death. So when Paul does refer to the earthly Jesus, it is more often than not to the climax of his life—namely, his death and resurrection (e.g., Gal. 3:10–14; 1 Cor. 2:1–4; 15:1–58; 2 Cor. 5:11–21; Rom. 3:21–31). Another way to make this same point is to observe that Paul, like the other New Testament writers, saw in the events of the cross, the empty tomb, the exaltation, and

Christ's sending of the Spirit at Pentecost the inauguration of a new era in redemptive history. After Pentecost, there were far more important things to teach about Jesus than just the course of his earthly ministry in Israel, significant though that was.[49]

Fifth, as the next main section will show, there is widespread continuity between Jesus and Paul on broader theological topics, presupposing an extensive knowledge of the Jesus tradition even when quotations, allusions, or echoes are not explicitly present. The more one agrees with the current scholarly trend to recognize Paul as steeped in early Jewish Christian rather than late Hellenistic backgrounds, the more this conclusion naturally follows.[50]

Sixth, the very sense of divine guidance or inspiration that gave Paul the freedom to claim every bit as authoritative an apostolic ministry as the leaders of the church in Jerusalem had (see esp. Galatians 1–2; 1 Corinthians 9; 2 Corinthians 10–13) also gave him the freedom to write things up in his own words. If he could cite or allude to the Old Testament without being bound by its strict wording or original meaning in many instances, because of his sense of what God was saying through the text to his people in a new age, he could surely promulgate authoritative doctrine and ethical behavior without woodenly citing the words of Jesus at every turn. And even when he did refer to Jesus' words, they formed a "*living* tradition, tradition which was evidently adaptable to different needs and diverse contexts" in a form "not yet finally fixed."[51] Indeed, it is possible that the traditions of Jesus' words themselves existed in two separate forms, one more fixed due to specific usage (like the liturgical tradition of the Last Supper), and another, probably much larger, more fluid collection, by analogy with Jewish treatments of written and oral Torah, respectively.[52]

Seventh, to whatever extent the Jerusalem apostles or emissaries claiming to represent them *did* stress their personal ties with the historical Jesus (Acts 15; Galatians 1–2), ties Paul knew he could not match, he may have consciously chosen as well to distance himself somewhat from the tradition of Jesus' earthly words and works. Only by focusing instead on his direct encounter with the risen Lord and subsequent calling and commissioning by him could Paul hope to convince people of the correctness of his message and of an equal authority to promote it.

In short, however one assesses the extent to which Paul was

aware of and utilized the Jesus tradition, there are numerous reasons why we do not see it appearing more frequently and more
explicitly in his epistles. But it is perhaps easier to *underestimate*
than to overestimate how much does in fact appear and how
much Paul actually knew.

Broader Theological Comparisons

At least as important as the question of Paul's specific knowledge
of Jesus' life is the issue of his congruence with Jesus' thought.
Perhaps Paul did have a fairly detailed knowledge of the historical Jesus, but that does not ensure that he agreed with him! To assess the claims that Paul was the true founder (or at least a second
founder) of Christianity, we must also compare what the two individuals taught and believed as central to their religious understanding. Here, of course, we return to the vexed question of what
portions of the Gospels may be accepted as authentic Jesus material. The previous chapter has made a powerful case for accepting
large portions of that material, but that is still different from arguing for the authenticity of individual sayings and deeds. In the following survey, therefore, I largely limit myself to features of the
Gospel tradition that are widely held to be historical. This means
that most of my comparisons will be with the central contours of
the Synoptic Gospels rather than with John, despite the possibility
of arguing for John's trustworthiness (see above, p. 29). It also
means that I will be making my comparisons with elements of the
tradition accepted by a broad, centrist consensus of scholars, not
restricting myself to the very truncated picture of the Jesus Seminar (again, see above, pp. 18–19). Where I rely on details more
widely doubted, I cite specific studies that have convinced me of
the authenticity of those details, even if they represent minority
voices. As for Paul, we can largely rely on the seven undisputed
letters (Galatians, 1 Thessalonians, 1 and 2 Corinthians, Romans,
Philippians, and Philemon) and still have an adequate sampling
of his key themes.[53]

JUSTIFICATION BY FAITH AND THE KINGDOM OF GOD

Few would dispute that a central theme of Paul's theology involves justification by faith—becoming right with God not
through works of the Law but through sheer trust in Christ's

mercy and grace (see esp. Galatians 1–4 and Romans 1–5). Even fewer would disagree with the claim that the present and future kingdom of God formed *the* heart of the proclamation of Jesus. Surely this example alone shows how far removed Paul was from Jesus. In fact, a closer look at both concepts reveals precisely the opposite.

"Justification" was a common legal metaphor in the first-century Greco-Roman world for the acquittal of a person before a court of law. When Paul declares that humans become right with God only by faith and not by legal works, he is building on that metaphorical usage of "justification," or *dikaiosunē* in Greek. But the word also carries the sense of "righteousness." Theologically, Paul stresses that God "imputes" Christ's righteousness to us when we trust in him for our salvation. Thus our heavenly Father looks at us and sees not our sinful natures but Jesus' sinless nature. Only in this way are we "cleared" to stand before and live in the presence of a perfectly righteous and holy God.

But God's "righteousness" refers not merely to his holiness but also to his justice. In fact there is no separate word in the Greek of Paul's letters that means "justice"; *dikaiosunē* and cognates do double duty for both concepts. We should reread our English translations and substitute "justice" whenever we see the word "righteousness" to determine what additional meaning may be present. Then we will recognize that God not only "imputes" to us a new standing before him but gives us the responsibility, and the empowerment "in Christ," to begin to implement his righteous standards in our lives and in this world.[54]

Suddenly, "justification" does not seem nearly so far removed from Jesus' notion of the kingdom of God. The Greek word for "kingdom" is *basileia*, translating an underlying Hebrew *malkuth*. In both languages, "kingdom" refers more to a power than to a place, more to a reign than to a realm. "Kingship" might better render the concept in English or, as Ben Witherington likes to translate it, "the dominion of God."[55] When we observe the largely synonymous parallelism in the Lord's Prayer, "Your kingdom come; your will be done on earth as it is in heaven" (Matt. 6:10), we recognize that God inaugurates his kingdom on earth in order for his righteous standards to affect the behavior of his subjects individually, corporately, and, to the extent that they can provide salt and light for society (Matt. 5:13–16), even to transform a corrupt world. Paul may have used an entirely different expression much better known to the Greeks and Romans among whom he largely ministered than the very Jewish, theocratic notion of God's reign, but he has hardly distorted the spirit of Jesus' proclamation.

Moreover, Paul does continue to refer to "the kingdom of God," even if not nearly as often as Jesus did. And these references reflect the same basic range of present and future dimensions of the kingdom as found in the Gospels (compare, respectively, 1 Cor. 4:20–21; Rom. 14:17; and Col. 4:10; with 2 Thess. 1:5–12, esp. v. 5; 1 Thess. 2:11–12; Gal. 5:21; 1 Cor. 6:9–10 and 15:50).[56] Conversely, Jesus talks about "faith" as fundamental for a person's response to himself in numerous places, particularly striking in his fourfold use of the slogan "your faith has saved you [or "made you well"]" in Mark 5:34 and parallels, Mark 10:52 and parallel, Luke 7:50 and 17:19.[57] Admittedly, the *dikai-* word-group is not as common. "Righteousness" as a noun appears mostly in Matthew to refer to right behavior, while the rare uses of "justify" as a verb in the Gospels usually mean "to vindicate." But Luke 18:14 concludes the parable of the Pharisee and the tax collector with Jesus' pronouncement that the latter went home "justified" rather than the former. The verb is identical in both form and meaning to Paul's favorite usage. And the tax collector's prayer to God—literally, "be propitiated concerning me"—employs the verb that is cognate to the key Pauline term *hilastērion* for an atoning sacrifice that appeases God's wrath (cf. Rom. 3:25). Combine all this with the imagery of the tax collector praying from a posture of utter dependence on God rather than self, acknowledging his abject sinfulness, and we should not be surprised when F. F. Bruce declares this parable one of the most "Pauline" pieces of teaching found in the Gospels.[58]

In incorporating a significant portion of Jesus' emphases in his use of "justification by faith," Paul is making no more drastic a change of terminology than John does when he, too, uses "kingdom" very rarely (only in John 3:3, 5, and 18:36), but regularly substitutes "eternal life" for the same idea in addressing his much more Hellenistic audience.[59] In fact, Matthew's account of Jesus' dialogue with the rich young ruler shows how interchangeable several terms had become in early Christian thinking.

The young man asks, "What good thing must I do to get *eternal life?*" (Matt. 19:16), Jesus replies in terms of entering both the *kingdom of heaven* and the *kingdom of God* (vv. 23, 24), and the disciples follow up with their question about who can be *saved* (v. 25)—the most common contemporary evangelical term for the process!

THE ROLE OF THE LAW

No theological topic among the teachings of Jesus and Paul has generated recent scholarly interest more than their treatment of the Old Testament Law. Clearly neither individual believed that the Law could "save" a person. But neither did either man jettison any portion of the Hebrew Scriptures as irrelevant or no longer authoritative for believers. In between these two extremes, however, both teachers have been accused at best of being at odds with each other and at worst of contradicting themselves.[60] Yet again, a closer look reveals much more that Jesus and Paul have in common.

Since the Reformation, Protestant interpreters have acknowledged three main purposes for the Law in Paul's thinking—pointing out the extent of human sin and thus the need of a savior, deterring sin to prevent it from becoming even more pervasive, and functioning as a moral (but not civil or ceremonial) guide for Christian behavior. All three of these purposes can be found in Galatians alone (see 3:19–20; 3:21–4:7; and 5:13–26, respectively) and frequently elsewhere (most notably Romans 4–7). Often Protestant interpreters have missed important distinctions between Jesus and Paul and interpreted teaching like Christ's Sermon on the Mount as if Paul had written it, and as if it reflected impossible legal demands designed to drive us to our knees to trust in Jesus and to abandon attempts to obey the Law. For the most part, however, Jesus does not enjoin ethical behavior in keeping with Paul's first two uses of the Law.

On the other hand, there is considerable overlap between Jesus' appeal to legal Scriptures and Paul's third use of the Law (or *tertius usus legis* as the Reformers called it). Matthew 5:17–20 encapsulates Jesus' primary understanding of the function of the Law in light of his coming: "Do not think that I have come to abolish the Law or the Prophets; I have not come to abolish them but to fulfill them." All of the Christian "Old Testament" remains an authority for Jesus, but at the same time he does not merely accept the status quo. "Fulfilling" the Law, as illustrated in the subsequent "antitheses" of the Sermon on the Mount (5:21–48), means that Christ has become the Law's sovereign interpreter, sometimes internalizing or radicalizing it, sometimes transcending or superseding it, but by no means leaving it unchanged.[61] Precisely because he is inaugurating the kingdom age, his followers will have to understand how his incarnation, teaching, death, and resurrection redefine God's will for a new era of human history.

Interestingly, Paul uses the identical verb in his summary statement in Galatians 5:14: "For the entire law is *fulfilled* in keeping this one command: 'Love your neighbor as yourself.'" Paul repeats it again a few verses later in 6:2: "Carry each other's burdens and in this way you will *fulfill* the Law of Christ." The expression "Law of Christ" appears again in 1 Corinthians 9 as in some way equivalent to "God's Law for the Christian age," when Paul describes how he tries to be all things to all people so that by all means he might save some (vv. 19–23). But, in becoming like one not having the Law of Moses in ministering among Gentiles, he is "not free from God's law but [is] under Christ's law" (v. 21). A lot of ink has been spilled discussing what Paul meant by "Christ's Law," but the best synthesis probably is "the Law as it has been taken in hand by Christ himself,"[62] including both Jesus' own enunciation of the gospel message and Jesus' understanding of the Old Testament as fulfilled in him.

A more detailed consideration of both Jesus and Paul on the topic of the Law can show them to be in fundamental agreement with each other on a number of points.[63] Here I note only four significant examples, all of which contrast sharply with the common forms of Judaism in their day.

To begin, both Jesus and Paul recognize the abiding authority of what has often been called the moral law—fundamental Old Testament ethical principles such as love of God and neighbor, honoring parents, respecting life and property, sexual relations reserved for monogamous, heterosexual marriage, and so on. Neither, however, sets apart the "Ten Commandments" (Exodus 20) as somehow distinct from all the rest. In fact, both Jesus and Paul recognize that the Sabbath commandment will not continue unchanged into the new age. Jesus not only challenges the Pharisaic traditions of what counted as work on the Sabbath; he outlines a principle which, if fully implemented, would altogether do away with the practice of ceasing from labor one day in seven: "The Sabbath was made for people, not people for the Sabbath," so that it is always lawful "to do good" on the Sabbath (Mark 2:27; 3:4 par.). So, too, Paul, if we may accept the testimony of Colossians 2:16–17, links the Sabbath with monthly and annual festivals of the Jews that "are a shadow of the things that were to come; the reality, however, is found in Christ." Until the emperor Constantine legalized Sunday as a day off work in the early 300s, Christians fairly uniformly agreed that resting one day in seven reflected heretical "Judaizing"![64]

Second, while both Jesus and Paul quoted the command to honor father and mother and recognized its abiding application in various contexts (Mark 7:9–13 par.; Eph. 6:2–3), both proved highly countercultural as single men in a Jewish culture that virtually required marriage of healthy adult males, especially religious leaders. Both also promoted certain values that could hardly be called "pro-family" in our current political environment (Luke 14:26; 1 Cor. 7:8, 26–27, 32–35, 38, 40). More generally, both exhibited definite ascetic tendencies, even while not going to the extremes of some Hellenistic philosophers in demanding them.[65]

Third, both challenged conventional Jewish thinking by predicting the demise of the current temple and/or sacrificial system, to be replaced by a spiritualized equivalent. Jesus explicitly envisioned the razing of all the temple's stones, as literally occurred in A.D. 70 (Mark 13:2 par.), while Paul imagined the supersession of animal sacrifices in Christ's "Paschal" sacrifice (e.g., 1 Cor. 5:7). For Jesus, the fulfillment of the sacrificial laws occurred in the "temple" which was his body (John 2:19);[66] derivatively, Paul could call believers corporately and individually God's temple (1 Cor. 3:16–17; 6:19).

Fourth, both men recognized the dietary laws, even as commanded in the Old Testament, to be superseded in Christ. Jesus set the stage for this development himself in Mark 7:14–22 and parallel, in which he contrasted what went into one's body (that did *not* defile a person) with what came out of one's body (that *could* defile a person). Perhaps writing with "20/20 hindsight,"

Mark adds the parenthetical comment in 7:19b that "in saying this, Jesus declared all foods clean." Paul likewise recognizes food as one of the morally neutral matters about which some Christians still have scruples, while others feel free to eat anything. In 1 Corinthians 8–10, the issue is probably the pagan practice of eating meat sacrificed to idols, but in Romans 14–15 it is more likely the Jewish dietary laws that are in view. Philippians 3:18–19 may similarly refer to those who mandate keeping a kosher table— "their god is their stomach"![67]

THE GENTILE MISSION AND THE CHURCH

If obeying the Law of Moses were not a prerequisite for salvation, then Gentiles could come to Christ far more easily than if it were. The next natural topic to discuss, then, in comparing Jesus and Paul, involves their conception of the nature and makeup of the community of believers. A century ago, the radical French Catholic scholar Alfred Loisy issued a declaration that has often been cited and believed: "Jesus foretold the kingdom of God, but it was the church that came."[68] Rephrased in terms of the discussion of "Jesus versus Paul," it can be alleged that Jesus did not envision the church, so that Paul's central focus on the church offers further proof of how far he deviated from Jesus. Not only this, but Jesus ministered almost exclusively to Jews, while Paul preached predominantly to Gentiles, creating a movement of people from a diversity of backgrounds that Jesus never imagined.

Once again, though, more careful scrutiny gives the lie to these simplistic generalizations. Although they appear only in Matthew, there are numerous evidences of Semitisms in the three Gospel texts that use the word "church" (*ekklēsia*) (Matt. 16:18; 18:17 [twice]), suggesting that that they may indeed go back to Jesus.[69] In these promises of a church emerging out of the band of his twelve closest followers, we are not to envision the highly structured, organized institution of the second century and beyond. Rather, behind the Greek word *ekklēsia* probably lies the Hebrew *qāhāl*, the standard term for the "assembly" of God's people in Old Testament times. But, as in that assembly, which eventually developed into the Jewish synagogues, there would have been some structure, at least in individual congregations, indeed as already was present among the Twelve (with Peter,

James, and John designated as an inner core of leadership), from the very beginning.[70]

More broadly, much of Jesus' ethical teaching presupposes a community of his followers living for a significant period of time in this fallen world, having to cope with its many hardships—exactly what came to be called "the church." Thus Jesus teaches about marriage and divorce (Mark 10:1–12 par.), about civil taxes (Mark 12:13–17 par.), about dealing with the hostilities of an occupying military force (Matt. 5:41), about legal matters and going to court (Matt. 5:25–26, 33, 39), and about a coming persecution for one's Christian allegiance (Mark 13:9–11 par.). The Synoptic Gospels devote even greater detail to Jesus' teaching about stewardship in general and money in particular.[71] Not surprisingly it is on precisely these topics where Paul tends to refer to Jesus' teaching the most (see above, pp. 74–76). Conversely, one must not read too much structure (as in later centuries) into Paul's discussions of the church, particularly in his undisputed letters. First Corinthians 14:26–40, for example, describes a fairly "charismatic" community, with each believer gifted in one or more ways, having opportunities to share those gifts when each local house-church gathered for worship.

It is equally inaccurate to claim that Jesus never envisioned a Gentile mission. Unless one is prepared to decimate the Synoptic tradition and label almost all of it inauthentic, at times for no other reason than the circular one that Jesus could not have imagined incorporating Gentiles into his movement, there is abundant evidence that he laid the groundwork for precisely such a development. His unusual concern for the outcasts of his society—the poor, women, the sick, the ritually impure, and most notably Samaritans[72]—though not always going beyond the bounds of Israel or Judaism, certainly paved the way for the Gentile mission. His command to love one's enemies (Matt. 5:44) sets the stage for the same. His commendation of the Gentile centurion as having more faith than anyone he had seen in Israel passes the "dissimilarity test"[73] for authenticity with flying colors and would have shocked a conventional Jewish audience. And his actual "withdrawal" from Galilee and ministry among Gentiles (Mark 7:24–8:10 par.) surely shows his concern for all peoples, even if his ministry largely followed the pattern which Paul himself would later enunciate and imitate of going "to the Jew first" and then also "to the Greek" (Rom. 1:16).[74]

Nor were these two missions conducted in splendid isolation from each other. Even before the more disputed letters like Ephesians and Colossians, the unity of Jew and Gentile in Christ was a prevailing passion of Paul's (see esp. Romans 9–11). Even if he could not look back to an identical phenomenon during Christ's lifetime, enough precedent had been established to make the development natural. Wedderburn well summarizes: "Just as Jesus, as God's representative, had signified God's acceptance of sinners by eating with them, so now too God was signifying acceptance of Gentile sinners by pouring out the divine Spirit upon them as upon Jewish Christians."[75] Or as John Barclay phrases it, "For both Jesus and Paul, the core of the good news consists in the radical demolition of restrictive boundaries in the free and gracious activity of a merciful God."[76]

Similarly, several of Jesus' corporate metaphors for his followers—for example, "the little flock" (Luke 12:32) of previously "lost sheep" (Luke 15:3–7 par.), or a new family with ties closer than those to biological kin (Mark 3:31–35 par.)—may well have inspired Paul's frequent depiction of the church as a "body," particularly "the body of Christ" (see esp. 1 Corinthians 12). A body requires a head (Jesus), just as a flock had a lead shepherd and a family in the first century had husband and father as highest authority. Similarly, Paul's favorite "in Christ" metaphor suggests an organic, collective connection between Jesus and his followers that built on their close, earthly relationship as a band of intimate associates. Paul may have even had Jesus' teaching about the Eucharist representing his body in mind (cf. Mark 14:22 par. with 1 Cor. 11:27, 29). Both teachers clearly envisioned the creation of a close-knit group of believers, corporately or communally carrying out their assigned tasks. As Wenham sums up, "Jesus may not have seen himself as founding the church as we think of it today, but he did see himself as gathering together the saved people of God."[77] And more than ever before these people would come from all the ethnic groups of the world.

The Role of Women

Closely related to the communal life of early Christians breaking down barriers between Jew and Gentile is the emphasis placed by both Jesus and Paul on a prominent role for women, at least by the cultural standards of their day. Potentially the most scandalous aspect of Jesus' relationships with women was his allowing a group of them literally to travel with him and with his male followers during his itinerant ministry, despite the suspicions of immorality that such a troupe would inevitably have generated (Luke 8:1–3). In allowing Mary of Bethany to "sit at his feet" and learn from his teaching (10:39), he was welcoming her functioning in a capacity as a student of Torah, precisely the role usually forbidden to women by orthodox Judaism in the first century. And he not only permitted Mary's behavior, he praised it and rebuked her sister Martha for being preoccupied with conventional domestic roles (vv. 41–42). On the other hand, Jesus stopped just short of unambiguously promoting full-fledged egalitarian relations between the genders, as he more exclusively chose men to form his group of twelve closest followers.[78]

Paul, too, shows unusual openness to women leaders in his churches. He frequently includes women's names among his "co-workers" (see esp. the greetings in Rom. 16:3–16 and Phil. 4:2–3). He recognizes that all the spiritual gifts God gives are for all believers exactly as the Spirit chooses to distribute them (1 Cor. 12:7–11). Among these are the gifts of prophet, pastor, and teacher, though these do not necessarily correspond to the formal roles (sometimes called "offices") that may bear the same name. Even more strikingly, Paul envisions women *apostles* ("missionaries" or "church planters"—Rom. 16:7) and *deacons* (Rom. 16:1). Yet, like Jesus, Paul also draws a line and excludes the role or office of overseer/elder from women, apparently the "highest" level of authority in his churches (1 Tim. 2:12). In today's churches, this role is often the functional equivalent of a senior pastor in a multiple-staff church or the sole pastor in a single-staff congregation.[79]

CHRISTOLOGY

Probably most controversial of all, Jesus is often said not to have had overly exalted views of himself, whereas Paul, more than anyone else in early Christianity, turned him into the Christ, the Son of God, and the divine Lord, equal in some respect to Yahweh, God of Israel, himself. Once again, here also one has to jettison not merely the Gospel of John but also large swaths of the Synoptic tradition in order to defend such sweeping generalizations. Interestingly, however, even if we limit ourselves to considering a cross section of the most commonly accepted material from the Synoptics, extensive "implicit christology" emerges. In other words, there are numerous hints in Jesus' teaching and behavior, completely apart from his alleged use of specific exalted titles for himself, that suggest he thought of himself as more than just another Jewish rabbi or prophet.

The Implicit Christology of the Synoptics

We may list no less than thirteen phenomena that fall into this category, including symbolic actions, key relationships, and other miscellaneous features.[80]

SYMBOLIC ACTIONS

1. It is widely agreed that Jesus' baptism is a historical fact, since it creates the potential embarrassment of Jesus having submitted to a rite that John proclaimed as symbolizing the forgiveness of sins.[81] But it is precisely at this event, at the inauguration of Jesus' public ministry, that he hears a heavenly voice combining excerpts of Psalm 2:7 and Isaiah 42:1 and declaring, "This is my Son, whom I love; with him I am well pleased." Whatever the reality behind this seemingly supernatural event, Jesus likely believed himself to be the fulfillment of these texts' prophecies about a coming messianic Son and Suffering Servant.

2. While scholars differ on how miracles were accomplished, a growing consensus accepts that the historical Jesus was perceived as working miracles, especially physical healings and exorcisms. It is also widely agreed that the central point of this miracle-working activity was to demonstrate the arrival of the kingdom of God, the messianic era (see esp. Matt. 12:28 par.).[82] But if the messianic age had arrived, then the Messiah must have come. A new kingdom requires a newly enthroned king.

3. The poorly named "triumphal entry" on what we call Palm Sunday clearly showed Jesus enacting the fulfillment of a messianic prophecy—the king coming on a donkey (Zech. 9:9). The crowds' adulation demonstrated that they recognized this claim; what they did not recognize was that Jesus came in peace, to die, not to overthrow the Romans and rule from a literal throne in Jerusalem (Mark 11:1–11 par.).

4. The closely related "temple clearing" (Mark 11:15–19 par.)

symbolically predicts the temple's destruction, which Jesus will explicitly forecast a day or two later (Mark 13:2 par.).[83] But without a temple, there would be no place to carry out the Old Testament's prescribed animal sacrifices for the forgiveness of sins. Jesus must have imagined some other system being put in place, which only someone very closely related to God could authorize, since the sacrificial laws of Scripture were originally presented as inviolable.

5. Jesus hints at that new system in his "words of institution" during the Last Supper. Viewing the cup of wine as symbolic for his coming death, he declares, "This is my blood of the covenant, which is poured out for many" (Mark 14:24 par.). While he does not elaborate, here are the raw data for the Epistle to the Hebrews' much more elaborate and theological reflection on Christ as the once-for-all sacrifice for human sin.[84]

Key Relationships

6. If John the Baptist was the last and greatest of the Old Testament–era prophets, Jesus must have been someone greater (or at least thought himself to be someone greater). After all, he declares "the least in the kingdom of heaven" to be "greater than" John (Matt. 11:11 par.). He also alludes to himself in declaring elsewhere that "one greater than Jonah" and "one greater than Solomon is here" (Matt. 12:41–42 par.).

7. Jesus' relationships with the Jewish leaders also disclose stunningly audacious claims. Precisely because Jesus challenged not only Pharisaic tradition but the ongoing applicability, at least at a literal level, of such fundamental Old Testament commands as Sabbath observance, temple worship, and the dietary laws, he must be viewed as transitioning between eras of redemptive history in ways permitted only to God.[85]

8. By calling twelve disciples, Jesus was forming the nucleus of a new or freed Israel (see esp. Matt. 19:28).[86] No longer would ethnicity imply election, but God's people would be made up of those of any nation or race who became Christ's disciples. But again the question arises, who besides God has the authority to institute such changes?

Other Features

9. On more than one occasion, Jesus claims that God's response to humans on judgment day will be based on their responses to

Jesus in this life (Mark 8:38 par.; Matt. 10:32–33; Luke 12:8–9). But previous revelation gives no mere mortal the privilege of functioning as such a "filter" in divine judgment!

10. So, too, the manner in which Jesus claims the authority to forgive sins goes well beyond the function of the Jewish priesthood, as the Jewish leaders who listen to his claims recognize (see esp. Mark 2:1–12 par.).

11. On numerous occasions, Jesus employs metaphors for himself that are commonly used in the Old Testament for Yahweh alone. These metaphors occur especially frequently in parables that contain a master figure whose behavior justifies activity that Jesus is being questioned about (see, e.g., Luke 15:3–7, 8–10, and 11–32). Individually, none of these metaphors necessarily proves all that striking, but together they form a strong case that Jesus saw himself as a unique earthly representative of Yahweh, functioning exactly as the God of Israel did throughout the Hebrew Bible. These roles include a bridegroom, rock, director of the harvest, shepherd, sower, vineyard owner, dispenser of forgiveness, father, king, and one who receives children's praise (Matt. 21:16).[87]

12. Jesus' use of the Aramaic term *Abba* for Father in addressing God reflects an unusual intimacy not common among first-century Jews. The term is explicitly reproduced in Greek transliteration in Mark 14:32 and thus presumably underlies other uses of "father" by Jesus in the Gospels, even when the Gospel writers translate Jesus' words with the more standard Greek *patēr*.[88]

13. Finally, even as simple-sounding a term as *amēn*, used by itself (or doubled, as consistently in John), introduces dozens of Jesus' declarations, giving them a remarkable air of authority. The term is usually translated something like "truly" in English. But it deviates from standard rabbinic patterns of justifying one's teaching by appeals either to Scripture or to previous rabbis' pronouncements. Jesus employs neither of these techniques. He does not even follow the model of the prophets by declaring, "Thus says the Lord . . ." Instead, he simply but sovereignly announces, "Truly I say to you," as if he needed no further justification for his solemn and sweeping statements. Only one believing he had some kind of divine authority would speak in this fashion.

More Explicit Christology

Once one realizes how widely *implicit* christology appears in the core of Synoptic material broadly accepted as authentic, the move to more *explicit* titles for Christ seems much more natural. In addition, it is easier to believe that their use in the Gospels is historically accurate. Even if we focus just on the four key titles that link the Gospels and Paul, we can make a case for more continuity than discontinuity between the teachings of these two men.

The most obviously authentic title that represented Jesus' favorite form of self-description was Son of Man. But this is one title that does *not* appear in Paul's writings.[89] Still, "Son" and "Son of God" do. And when one investigates the background to Jesus' use of "Son of Man," one discovers that it meant far more than "merely human"—as, for example, frequently in Ezekiel when God addresses the prophet with that expression. Rather, the most relevant background appears in Daniel 7:13, in which one "like a son of man" is ushered into the very presence of God and promised universal dominion over the nations of the world. When one recognizes that "Son of God" in Jewish backgrounds likewise often denoted an exalted messiah, not the ontologically co-equal second person of the Trinity as in later Christian theologizing, then the titles "Son of Man" and "Son of God" prove more like each other than different.[90] Probably Jesus' use of *Abba* (see above, p. 100) forms an important bridge between the two titles and also an important reason why, even in the Gospels, "Son" and "Son of God" began to take on even *more* exalted overtones. One who was specially conscious of an unparalleled filial intimacy with Yahweh would be a uniquely divine Son of God.[91] Interestingly, the one other New Testament writer outside of the Gospels who preserves *Abba* in Greek transliteration is Paul (Rom. 8:15; Gal. 4:6), who views the term as an appropriate title for believers to use in addressing their adoptive heavenly Father. The use is so unusual that Paul must have based it, perhaps already with Jewish Christian precedent, on the Jesus tradition itself.

The use of "Christ" or "Messiah" forms a second fairly direct link between Jesus and Paul. Although it was not his preferred way of describing himself, because so many Jews were looking for a militaristic messiah who would overthrow the Romans, Jesus nevertheless tacitly acknowledged it as an accurate label at key junctures in his ministry (most notably Mark 8:29 par.; 14:62 par.). Paul too recognizes it as an appropriate label for Jesus, particularly in Romans 9:5 where commentators are agreed the titular sense remains. Many scholars think the majority of uses in Paul merely reflect the beginnings of the later trend to turn "Christ" into a proper name, but I have argued elsewhere that this is not the case.[92] At any rate, both Jesus and Paul recognize that there are legitimate ways in which Jesus can be called the messianic deliverer of Israel.

A third frequent title for Jesus in both the Gospels and Paul is "Lord." Striking here is the twofold Jewish and Old Testament background, whereby the Greek *kurios* regularly translated the divine name of Yahweh in the Septuagint. Not every usage in the Gospels by any means reflects this strong a sense. Many people addressed Jesus as Lord simply as a title of respect, somewhat equivalent to "Master" in the days of servants or slaves in English-speaking countries. But in some contexts, the term seems stronger than that (see esp. Matt. 14:28 or Luke 5:8). And in Mark 12:35–37 and parallels, Jesus himself referred to the Messiah as "Lord," in a context that directly challenged conventional Jewish expectations that the Messiah would be a *merely* human descendant of David.[93] Conversely, Paul recognizes that *kurios* means master as well as God, as classically in the early Christian confession of Romans 10:9—"Jesus is Lord." Set against a backdrop of increasingly outrageous claims by and for the emperor as absolute human master as well as divine, Christians at times risked their lives by elevating Jesus, and Jesus alone, to this position.

Far less common in the Synoptic Gospels but still important, especially for Matthew, is "Son of David," a term that clearly links with "Messiah" because of the Messiah's expected Davidic ancestry. A key passage in Paul that demonstrates knowledge of this expectation is Romans 1:3, which describes the "Son" with respect to his "earthly life" as "a descendant of David." So while distinctive christologies obviously appear when one compares Paul with the Synoptics, just as they do when one compares each of the four Gospels with the others, it is hardly accurate to say that Paul took the picture of a simple Jewish prophet or rabbi and distorted it into an exalted, divine figure contrary to the actual historical evidence about what Jesus did and said.[94]

ESCHATOLOGY

A natural topic with which to conclude our theological survey is eschatology. How similar were Jesus' and Paul's teachings about the end of the world? As it turns out there is considerable overlap. And the appropriate place to start with eschatology is at Christ's death, since, as already seen in my survey of "kingdom" teaching, both Jesus and Paul believed that the last days (the presence of the kingdom) began with Christ's death and resurrection.

Although it is fashionable to deny that Jesus predicted the future on any topic, a strong case can in fact be made that he foresaw his own death. Anyone who took the stances he did could have expected hostility from either or both of the Jewish and Roman leaders. His threefold "passion prediction" (Mark 8:31 par.; 9:31 par.; 10:33–34 par.) leads to his claim that he came "to give his life as a ransom for many" (10:45 par.). Both the triple prophecy in general and the specific saying about the purpose of his death show numerous signs of authenticity.[95] But Paul's frequent metaphor of "redemption"—the price paid for a slave's freedom— comes from the same word-group as "ransom" here in the Gospels. Paul is merely unpacking in considerable detail, after the event, the meaning of the crucifixion that Christ himself foretold.

The passion predictions, however, also predict Christ's resurrection. If one eliminates the possibility of the supernatural as a presupposition, then of course one will reject such predictions and the narratives of the resurrection itself, with which each Gospel ends. But apart from this *a priori* exclusion, there are good reasons for accepting the resurrection traditions (see above, pp. 68–70), so that Paul is clearly building on Jesus' teaching and actions in stressing this theme (see esp. 1 Corinthians 15). But, drawing on the same Old Testament background of which Jesus would have been aware (most notably Dan. 12:2), Paul recognizes that one resurrection is inextricably bound up with the resurrection of all people, so that he can think of Jesus as the firstfruit or guarantee of the general resurrection (1 Cor. 15:20; cf. vv. 21–28).[96] And, over against Hellenistic belief primarily in just the immortality of souls, Jesus and Paul both agree that their hope is for a bodily resurrection (vv. 35–49; cf. the otherwise enigmatic scene in Matt. 27:51–53).

Resurrection, however, is not the end of the story. Even before his resurrection, Christ repeatedly promised he would return again in glory at the end of human history to usher in judgment day (see esp. Mark 13 par.). So, too, Paul teaches at length in several passages about Jesus' "second coming" (see esp. 1 Thess. 4:12–5:11; 2 Thess. 2:1–12). In these same texts, both men also prophesied that there would be "great tribulation" on earth just preceding Christ's return, involving intensified persecution of believers and God's wrath being unleashed on unbelievers. Yet at the same time, many would come to know the Lord during this period. Included among these appear to be a large number of ethnic Jews coming to faith in Jesus as Messiah, perhaps just before Christ's return (Matt. 23:39 par.; Rom. 11:25–26). And both Jesus and Paul agree that all the peoples of the world throughout human history will stand before God for judgment, as God separates them into only two categories—believers who will spend blissful eternity in his presence in the company of all the redeemed, and unbelievers who will be consciously separated from him and all things good forever (cf. esp. Matt. 25:31–46 with 1 Cor. 3:10–17).[97]

The Role of Paul's Conversion

Many times treatments of the relationship between Jesus and Paul begin rather than end with a look at Galatians 1. There Paul refers to his conversion and avows, "[T]he gospel I preached is not of human origin. I did not receive it from any human source, nor was I taught it; rather, I received it by revelation from Jesus Christ" (vv. 11–12). It is often assumed that this brief statement settles the debate—Paul knew next to nothing about Jesus! But that view cannot be sustained in light of the massive amount of evidence to the contrary, evidence I have been able only briefly to highlight in this chapter.

So what then *does* Paul mean by this statement? Clearly it was no Christian evangelist who led Paul to the Lord; it was his supernatural encounter with the risen Christ on the road to Damascus (Acts 9:1–19). Seyoon Kim has stressed how much of Paul's fundamental theology must have changed on the basis of this encounter. Clearly Paul's christology was overturned—Jesus was not an apostate whose followers threatened the well-being of Judaism but a heavenly Messiah. Jesus clearly *was* resurrected, which, as just noted above (p. 103), meant that the last days had begun. The messianic age was present, which would culminate in the resurrection of all people. But the messianic age was the era in which the Gentiles would come to God in droves, hence Paul's emphasis on mission to the Gentiles and the incorporation of Jew and Gentile into one body. And, of course, if Jesus was the true Messiah, then salvation came by faith in him and not by legal works, while the elect community of God's people was composed of those who were his followers from any ethnic background.[98]

Those theological affirmations all follow naturally from Jesus' revelation of himself to Paul. But beyond that, Paul needed to be taught the events of Jesus' earthly life just like any other new convert. Ananias would inevitably have presented a brief outline of what Paul most needed to know when he found him at his house in Damascus and prepared him for baptism (Acts 9:17–19). Paul would have learned even more during the next "several days" from other disciples in Damascus (v. 20). And for those suspicious of Acts' reliability, Paul's own autobiographical remarks in Galatians 1:18–20 concede that three years later he spent more than two weeks with Peter and James in Jerusalem "to get acquainted" (v. 18). The precise meaning of the verb here (Gk. *historēsai*) has been disputed. It may actually mean to "interview" or even "do historical research," but, even if not, Paul would have inevitably learned considerably more about Christian origins during this time.[99] As we saw earlier, in his letters Paul more than once speaks of passing on what was delivered to him by tradition (see above, pp. 62, 64), which suggests a pattern of catechetical instruction. And none of this need be viewed as contradicting Galatians 1:11–12, which describes merely the independent *foundations* of the central truths of Paul's understanding of the gospel.[100]

Conclusion

Was Paul the true founder of Christianity, or at least a key "second founder"? By no means. He knew a considerable amount about the life and teachings of the historical Jesus, and his central proclamation depended on the veracity of the death and resurrection of Christ, precisely as described in the Gospels and predicted by Jesus himself. Theological distinctives between the two men remain, and the differing purposes of the Gospels and the Epistles must be taken into account when assessing the reasons for why certain issues do or do not appear in each. But on numerous central topics the two find themselves in profound agreement. As Dale Allison forthrightly concludes, "[T]he persistent conviction that Paul knew next to nothing of the teaching of Jesus must be rejected. Jesus of Nazareth was not the faceless presupposition of Pauline theology. On the contrary, the tradition stemming from Jesus well served the apostle in his roles as pastor, theologian, and missionary."[101]

CHAPTER 3

How Is the Christian to Apply the New Testament to Life?

Most readers of the New Testament have at times run across outrageous applications of the text. Some have perhaps invented a few themselves. The supposedly true story is told of a woman in a difficult marriage who opened her Bible at random, when her eyes fell on the text of Ephesians 4:22 in the King James Version ("put off . . . the old man, which is corrupt according to the deceitful lusts"), and she took the verse as giving her permission to initiate a divorce! Most misapplications are not this extreme, but I have personally heard Christians cite Philippians 4:13 ("I can do everything through him who gives me strength"—NIV) as support for tackling a task for which everyone around them recognizes they are neither gifted nor called. By citing the verse out of context, they miss that Paul was speaking of being content in any and every socioeconomic bracket. So, too, I have heard believers take 1 Timothy 5:8 ("Anyone who does not provide for their relatives . . . has denied the faith and is worse than an unbeliever") as a command that husbands should be their families' primary breadwinner. They fail to observe that the context refers to adult children, of either gender, providing for needy, aged parents.

These examples demonstrate that valid application cannot be separated from legitimate interpretation. Until we know what a passage meant in its original historical and literary contexts, and until we have a reliable translation that reflects accurate meanings of words and sentences in that passage, we cannot determine how to apply it to our quite different contexts in the twenty-first century. Countless manuals abound for assisting the novice interpreter in the principles of biblical interpretation—"hermeneutics" as it is often called.[1] But not nearly as many books focus primarily on application.[2] I have elsewhere written on some of the important principles to be aware of while interpreting each portion of the New Testament according to the literary *genres* of its books (Gospels, Acts, Epistles, Apocalypse) and according to the smaller *forms* that appear within those books (e.g., parables, miracles, vice-lists, hymns and confessions, etc.).[3] I have also described a basic four-step process for legitimate biblical application, irrespective of the part of Scripture one is reading. In short, it involves (1) determining the original application(s) intended by the passage; (2) evaluating the level of specificity of those applications to see if they should be (or even can be) transferred across time and space to other audiences; (3) if not, identifying broader cross-cultural principles that the specific elements of the text reflect; and (4) finding appropriate contemporary applications that embody those principles. I also go on to provide some specific guidance for accomplishing step (2) in particular.[4]

Here I want to do something that is a cross between the two approaches I have previously adopted. I will proceed through the New Testament in its canonical sequence, genre by genre, commenting on distinctive principles for *application* at each stage along the way. The results will involve covering some of the same ground that I have traversed before, but in a different format, as well as introducing new material.

There is no comprehensive set of principles that one can formulate abstractly, apart from discussions of individual texts and forms, so my survey here can hope only to be representative. A particularly useful new commentary series inaugurated in 1994 can help the reader with further thinking about applications. By the middle of 2004 the NIV Application Commentaries will be available for all of the New Testament books, and the Old Testament volumes are rapidly appearing as well.[5] The unique format of this series is to proceed through a biblical book, taking passages of preachable length, and arranging comments on those passages into three sections labeled "Original Meaning," "Bridging Contexts," and "Contemporary Significance." The latter two sections are designed to occupy a substantial portion of the commentary on each text, as they help readers think methodologically about how to move from the ancient setting to the modern world and then to generate legitimate applications. As in any multiauthor series, some volumes prove better than others, but overall the quality of the commentaries that have appeared thus far is quite high. Other recent series that devote significant attention to exposition and application, with consistently accurate and helpful comments, include the Bible Speaks Today (on both Testaments) and the InterVarsity Press New Testament Commentary Series (only on the New Testament).[6] Serious students of Scripture will also want to consult these volumes or others like them[7] when trying to apply the New Testament to the modern world.

One final introductory comment is in order. It would be wrong to begin our survey of principles for application without stressing that large portions of the Bible remain very clear, even at a great distance of time and space from their original contexts. The Protestant Reformers regularly spoke of the "perspicuity" of Scripture in combating the medieval Catholic notion that the Bible required an elite class of interpreters (the clergy) to make sense of it. Of course, as long as the Bible was read in Latin in church while most Europeans no longer spoke that language, it *did* require special help! But Protestants have regularly emphasized that when the Bible is accurately translated into the native tongues of people in any part of our world, everything necessary for them to understand God's plan of salvation in Christ and the kind of Christian life he wants his followers to live becomes crystal clear. On the other hand, the Reformers never claimed that Scripture was equally perspicuous in every passage or on every topic. Numerous texts and themes continued (and continue today) to divide equally competent, godly interpreters. Here is where the discipline of hermeneutics comes into play.[8]

The Gospels

GENERAL CONSIDERATIONS

Luke and John each supplies explicit statements concerning his purpose in writing accounts of the ministry and message of Jesus. Luke explains that he wants Theophilus to "know the certainty of the things" he has been taught (Luke 1:4). John adds that he writes his Gospel so "that you may believe that Jesus is the Messiah, the Son of God, and that by believing you may have life in his name" (John 20:31). In each case, the Gospel writers may be referring *both* to an initial conversion experience *and* to growth in Christian faith.[9] Thus the most fundamental applications of a study of any or all of the Gospels involve people placing their trust in Jesus as their Lord and Savior and then continuing to follow him in life-long discipleship. After all, the Gospels clearly recognize that ultimately God will divide humanity into only two "camps"—those who will spend a blissful eternity with him and those who will endure an agonizing eternal separation from God and everything good (Matt. 25:31–46; John 5:28–29; Revelation 20–22). And the criterion for dividing people into these two groups will be how they have responded to Christians who have proclaimed the gospel and thus how they have responded to Christ himself (see also Mark 8:38 par.).

But what about all the rest of the rich detail in the Gospels? I now proceed sequentially through Matthew, commenting on specific literary forms or topics and the principles attached to them, illustrating primarily from that Gospel but incorporating a few examples from Mark, Luke, and John as well.

SPECIFIC PRINCIPLES

Genealogies

Matthew begins with one of the two genealogies of Jesus that the Gospels present (Matt. 1:1–17; cf. Luke 3:23–37). At least one key principle in applying these seemingly lifeless lists of names is to note how they differ from conventional genealogies of the day. Matthew's includes the names of five of the mothers, all of whom had births that were shrouded with the suspicion of illegitimacy. Here we find the first hint of a theme that will dominate much of the Gospels' narratives—Jesus' concern for social outcasts. In applying this theme, we must identify who contemporary counterparts might be and begin to treat them with similar compassion.[10] Luke's genealogy likewise stresses Jesus' full humanity and concern for all people by showing how his ancestry goes all the way back to the first man, Adam.

Birth Narratives

Matthew 1:18–2:23 forms one of two Gospel accounts of the events surrounding Christ's birth (cf. Luke 1:2–2:52). Interestingly, both stress how Jesus' coming fulfilled numerous prophecies (though Luke does so more allusively). Some of these fulfillments are reflected in the straightforward narrations of events once predicted that have now occurred; others are "typological"—seeing God's hand behind strikingly recurrent patterns of behavior at key junctures in the history of redemption. Whenever either kind of prophecy is fulfilled in the New Testament, believers can gain greater confidence that the as-yet-unfulfilled prophecies of Scripture (especially surrounding Christ's return and the end of the world) will likewise come to pass, and that God works in human lives with predictable, recognizable patterns of activity for which they should look.[11]

The Ministry of John the Baptist

Matthew 3 is one of several key chapters in the Gospels on the divinely anointed prophet who would prepare the way for the Messiah. If one word sums up the message of John's ministry, it would be "repent." The specific examples of what this looked like in John's world (e.g., Luke 3:10–14) remind us that biblical repentance includes far more than mental regret or verbal apology. It involves a 180-degree turn or change in behavior. Good works play a crucial role in the believer's life, not as a basis for salvation, but as a demonstration of it. These good works begin with baptism, which Jesus likewise models here (Matt. 3:13–16 par.), and go on to include obedience to everything he commands (Matt. 28:20).[12]

Jesus' Temptations

Matthew 4:1–11 forms one of three Gospel accounts of Jesus' temptation. The writer to the Hebrews best captures the primary timeless applications of this event for believers: "[B]ecause [Jesus] himself suffered when he was tempted, he is able to help those who are being tempted" (Heb. 2:18), and "we do not have a high priest who is unable to empathize with our weaknesses, but we have one who has been tempted in every way, just as we are—yet he did not sin. Let us then approach God's throne of grace with confidence, so that we may receive mercy and find grace to help us in our time of need" (4:15–16).

Calling and Instructing the Disciples

As Jesus' ministry in Galilee gets underway, Matthew summarizes it as involving preaching/teaching and healing. Jesus calls his first disciples and shortly thereafter teaches them (and larger crowds) with his famous Sermon on the Mount (Matt. 4:12–7:29). A number of important principles come into play in applying these or any other teachings of Jesus.

First, *one needs to distinguish what is explicitly directed only to the Twelve.* The majority of people who became Jesus' followers even during his lifetime did not instantly leave their occupations and literally go on the road to accompany Christ during his itinerant ministry (as with Peter and friends in 4:18–22). Conversion and discipleship for the majority involve trust in Jesus and adherence to his principles for living in their ordinary walks of life.[13]

Second, *one must distinguish situation-specific commands to the Twelve that were revoked* even for them *later in the Gospels.* When Jesus sent the Twelve out to minister without him, they were to go only to fellow Jews (10:5–6). But this was a temporary priority; the Great Commission would make it clear they were later to go to all ethnic groups (28:19). So, too, Jesus' mandate that the apostles rely on others for material support (10:9–12) was rescinded on the last night of his life (Luke 22:35–38), though many contemporary parachurch groups seem not to have noticed and still require their employees to raise all their own support!

Third, *one must observe what may never have been explicitly limited to the Twelve, nor formally revoked, but could not be followed by Christians living in later generations.* A classic example appears in Christ's Farewell Discourse as he promises to send the Holy Spirit as a Comforter and Advocate. In John 14:26, Jesus promises that this "Paraclete" (to anglicize the Greek term *paraklētos*) "will teach you all things and will remind you of everything I have said to you." Obviously God's Spirit could remind only those who had literally walked with Jesus in and around Israel. Others had not heard Jesus say anything to them. This prophecy came true as the apostles scattered around the world after Pentecost, preaching about Jesus and, for John, as he wrote his Gospel as well. But this verse may not be used by later Christians to justify allegations of new revelation to them on a par with inspired Scripture.[14]

Fourth, *we should be alert to metaphors or other figures of speech not meant to be taken literally.* Somewhere between 80 and 90 percent of Jesus' teaching is poetic in form, and poetry regularly employs metaphorical language. When Jesus tells those who lust that it would be better to gouge out their eyes than to lose their whole bodies in hell (Matt. 5:29), he is not literally commanding people to mutilate themselves. The blind, after all, can lust every bit as much as those with sight! Rather he is employing a vivid metaphor for taking drastic action to avoid temptation.[15] So, too, when Jesus tells those who give alms not to "let [their] right hand know what [their] left hand is doing" (6:3), he does not mean that Christians should not keep financial records and be accountable to others for their giving practices. Paul elsewhere enjoins scrupulous accountability (2 Cor. 8:16–9:5). Rather, believers must give "secretly" enough (Matt. 6:4) that they are not tempted to give out of the desire to receive human praise or adulation (v. 1).

Fifth, *understanding historical background often proves crucial in determining how literally to apply one of Christ's commands.* Countless well-intentioned Christian leaders have inappropriately subjected battered wives to continuous physical abuse by telling them to keep on submitting to their husbands' mistreatment, and citing Jesus' call to "turn the other cheek" (Matt. 5:49). But a "slap" on one's "right cheek" in a world in which most people were forced to be right-handed was not the aggressive blow of a boxer, but a backhanded "cuff" often used by a superior to insult a subordinate. It did not inflict significant bodily harm. The correct application of the passage, therefore, would be more along the lines of "don't trade insults or retaliate when mistreated," not "deliberately subject yourself to ongoing physical abuse"![16] Many of Jesus' sayings require similar understanding of the meaning of behavior or customs in his world that are often lost on audiences in different times and cultures.

On the other hand, it is equally possible to miss the *radical* nature of many of Christ's commands precisely because we are unfamiliar with historical background. Today we might read Jesus' insistence that we love God more than family members (Matt.

10:37) as an obvious religious truism, without realizing how shocking Jesus' allegiance to spiritual kin above biological family was (e.g., Mark 3:31–35 par.). After all, his Jewish culture considered allegiance to parents, siblings, and children more fundamental than any other human loyalties. Then, as with some Christians today, it was often assumed that loyalty to family members *was* God's will, even when their demands contradicted God's word. Jesus, however, directly disputes this assumption (see also Luke 9:57–62 par.).[17]

Finally, individual teachings of Jesus are often embedded in larger sermons or discourses that contain seemingly contradictory teachings. *In these instances, legitimate application must take both strands of teaching into account.* For example, Matthew 7:1 ("Do not judge or you too will be judged") is regularly taken out of context, often by non-Christians who throw it back in Christians' faces when they attempt to label certain behavior as sinful. But verses 3–5 clearly call on Jesus' followers to judge, in the sense of "assessing" what is right and wrong. These verses include the admonition that once one has appropriately dealt with sin in one's own life, one should help others rid their lives of sin. The range of meanings of the Greek word for "judge" in verse 1 suggests that what Christ is forbidding there is an overly "judgmental" spirit. There are still plenty of contemporary applications left even when the text is correctly understood![18] Thus, for example, believers must "judge" (i.e., discern) that homosexual practice is sinful and explain to others that the Bible consistently makes that clear, but they must not "judge" (i.e., condemn) those who struggle with the practice nor single out this particular sin as somehow meriting more disapproval than heterosexual sins.

So, too, unless Jesus flatly contradicts himself not once but twice in three consecutive passages, his call to Peter to forgive "seventy-seven times" (or "seventy times seven"—Matt. 18:21–22) must be tempered by his model of church discipline in verses 15–20 and by the parable of the unforgiving servant in verses 23–35. While Jesus never wants his followers to harbor grudges against those who have sinned against them, forgiveness in the full-orbed, biblical sense of restoration to right relationship with one another cannot occur unless the sinning party repents. God will judge the unrepentant harshly (vv. 23–35) and calls on believ-

ers to remove fellowship from those who refuse all other overtures at reconciliation (vv. 15–20).[19]

One last example reminds us that sometimes balancing verses
appear elsewhere than in the immediate context. Taken by itself,
Jesus' promise to give to those who ask, seek, and knock (Matt.
7:7–11) seems like a blank check, and misguided Christians
throughout church history have at times believed that Jesus guar-
antees health and wealth if we simply ask persistently enough.
But Jesus assumes that his audience will remember his teaching
one chapter earlier that, when they pray, they leave room for
God's will to override theirs (6:10). It is not too sophisticated a
hermeneutical principle to remember that all of the New Testament books were designed to be read in one sitting, so that listeners would apply what we call chapter 6 to a text in chapter 7!

Miracle Stories

Chapters 8–9 comprise Matthew's largest collection of accounts of
Jesus' miracles, which appear at numerous other points throughout the Gospels as well. Probably the most important principle to
keep in mind in applying these passages is that all of the miracles
were originally intended to demonstrate the presence of the kingdom and the arrival of the Messiah (see esp. Matt. 12:28 par.).[20]
Thus the miracles are not first of all about how God wants to meet
human needs through Christ (though he certainly does that), but
about how we are to recognize who Jesus is. Despite countless
messages on the stilling of the storm that have claimed that "Jesus
will still the storms of your lives, too," it remains a fact that many
times he does not remove us from "troubled waters," but preserves us safely in their midst (cf. 1 Cor. 10:13). The most important way to apply the miracle is rather to glorify Jesus, mirroring
the disciples' original reaction: "The men were amazed and
asked, 'What kind of man is this? Even the winds and the waves
obey him!'" (Matt. 8:27).

In similar fashion, one cannot turn to miracles of physical healing and assume that the application for us is that we, too, can be
guaranteed restored health after illness or injury. After all, eventually every one of us will have a terminal experience—namely,
death. Rather, as explicitly in the healing of the paralytic in Matthew 9:1–8 and parallels, Jesus performs miracles of physical heal-

ing to demonstrate his ability to make good on a more important promise that we can *always* count on—spiritual healing, starting with the forgiveness of our sins (vv. 4–6).

Proverbs and Pronouncement Stories

Scattered throughout the Gospels appear individual teachings of Jesus closely resembling Old Testament proverbs. For example, Matthew 9:12 and parallels describe Jesus declaring, "It is not the healthy who need a doctor, but the sick." The most important principle to keep in mind in applying proverbs is that they are generalizations about what is often true, not rigid principles that admit no exceptions. There were times in the ancient world, as there are today, when doctors advised otherwise healthy patients, but that was (and is) not their *primary* function. The same is true at the level of "spiritual medicine." So one should not conclude from this proverb that Christians should never turn to Jesus except when they sin, even though it remains true that atoning for our sins was the primary reason for Jesus' ministry.

In many instances, proverbs or other short, climactic sayings are embedded in what scholars have come to call "pronouncement stories."[21] These episodes brought Jesus into conflict with various Jewish authorities, so they are also referred to as "conflict" or "controversy stories." Matthew 12:1–8 and parallels afford an excellent example. Jesus and his followers are confronted by the Pharisees because they have "harvested" some grain from the fields in order to eat it on a Sabbath. Jesus appeals to various Old Testament precedents to justify his behavior but then succinctly sums up the matter, claiming that "the Son of Man is Lord of the Sabbath" (v. 8). Here is the most radical and climactic portion of the passage. Jesus alleges to be able to speak on behalf of God, declaring authoritatively the meaning and application for his day of one of the ten central commandments of Old Testament Law. Verses 9–13 provide a second illustration of Jesus defying Pharisaic Sabbath strictures. Little wonder, then, that "the Pharisees went out and plotted how they might kill" him (v. 13). In some Christian cultures today, believers will likewise raise the ire of their own leaders if they implement Jesus' principles and defy local, legalistic regulations about what can or cannot be done on Sunday. But faithfulness in applying these texts demands precisely such defiance, however tactful, even when it comes at a cost![22]

Parables

Matthew 13:1–52 introduces us to a series of eight parables. Perhaps no section of Scripture has generated as much interpretive debate over the years as the parables of Jesus. I have elsewhere chronicled the controversy concerning to what extent parables may be considered allegories, and I have defended the approach that one may typically deduce one main lesson from each main character in a given parable.[23] Applying these lessons may often be helped by "contemporizing" the narratives—retelling the stories by using modern characters and situations that faithfully reproduce the original impact that Jesus' parables would have had on his audiences. Many times the central shock value of the parables is lost today, because of centuries of their domestication. Even unbelievers today are convinced that a "Samaritan" is a "good guy," because we name hospitals and laws that protect people after "the good Samaritan." But in jumping to that conclusion, we miss entirely the original force of Jesus' parable (Luke 10:25–37), because the Samaritans were the hated enemies of ancient Jews. For contemporary audiences we need to tell a story about an American G.I. dying on the battlefield, being rescued by one of Saddam Hussein's crack troops (or some similar, shocking equivalent). In so doing, we will more clearly communicate the central lesson of the parable that even one's *enemy* is one's neighbor, as well as re-creating the original force of the narrative by applying it to an equivalent current situation.

Or consider a second parabolic example. Imagine a story about a practicing homosexual who recognizes his addiction to a sinful lifestyle and struggles to abandon it, though never being more than partially successful. Insert an account of an upstanding conservative evangelical pastor who profusely thanks God for all his blessings, including the fact that God has spared him from the worst social addictions regularly plaguing our society. Conclude with Jesus' verdict that under certain circumstances the first man might be saved and the second one lost. Now we have reenacted the shock value of Jesus' parable of the Pharisee and the tax collector (Luke 18:9–14), in a world in which everyone knew Pharisees were respected Jewish leaders faithfully seeking to obey the Law in every area of life while tax collectors were the hated traitors who had sold out to work (at least indirectly) for the occupying Roman Empire. The contemporization then invites listeners to think of other, perhaps even closer, equivalents in their world to both characters and to reconsider their attitudes toward each.[24]

Confession and Misunderstanding

The next several chapters of Matthew provide more examples of literary forms already discussed—particularly more miracles and controversy stories. In the middle of chapter 16, we reach a turning point both for Matthew's Gospel in particular and for Jesus' ministry as a whole. In sharp juxtaposition to one another, successive passages narrate Peter's supernaturally aided recognition of Jesus as the true Messiah (16:13–20 par.) as well as his inability to accept the prediction of Jesus' upcoming suffering and death (vv. 21–28 par.). Both parts prove crucial for contemporary application. On the one hand, we are reminded of the overall purpose of the Gospels—to bring men and women to a saving knowledge of Jesus Christ. Unless a person is drawn, like Peter, to confess Jesus correctly, no other applications of the New Testament matter very much, since that person remains lost in his or her sin. But simply professing to follow Jesus is inadequate, especially if one does so merely for personal gain. The path of true discipleship is the road to the cross—death to self, denial of the "triumphalism" that perverts the gospel into a formula for worldly success and prestige, and the willingness to lay down one's life for Christ should that prove necessary, even if it means an ignominious and agonizing death (the true meaning of taking up one's cross and following Jesus—v. 24).[25]

Symbolic Actions

Again subsequent chapters repeat forms already introduced. The primary new form that increasingly punctuates the account of Jesus moving ever nearer his execution is that of symbolic action or prophetic object lesson, a form well-known to first-century Jews from comparable actions dotting the prophetic ministries of Isaiah, Jeremiah, Ezekiel, Hosea, Amos, and Zechariah. Indeed, the first such example visibly enacts the prophecy of Zechariah

9:9, as Jesus enters Jerusalem on a donkey in seemingly triumphal procession with the adulation of the crowds surrounding him (Matt. 21:1–11 par.). They recognize his messianic claims but, like Peter, miss the significance of the humble beast of burden. What church history has come to call Christ's "triumphal entry" is better labeled an "atriumphal entry"![26] The same applications that derived from Peter's confession and misunderstanding recur here. The Messiah will one day return to liberate his people from earthly suffering, but until then discipleship may actually increase the chance of such suffering.

Several of Jesus' symbolic actions threaten God's judgment on Israel, and on Jerusalem in particular. Jesus' "temple tantrum" enacts God's coming destruction of the temple if its leadership does not repent.[27] Sandwiched around this event, at least in Mark's account (Mark 11:12–25), is Jesus' cursing of the fig tree. When we recognize that fig trees were a common Old Testament symbol for Israel, it appears likely a similar symbolism is intended here as well. Even the parables and "woes" that Jesus utters as his ministry in Jerusalem continues (Matt. 21:28–22:14; 23:1–36) pursue this theme of judgment further. Many who thought they were God's people turn out to be his opponents instead. Appropriate contemporary application will ask where in the visible church of Christ do similar reversals appear. Unfortunately, one does not have to look very hard to find parallels in most cultures in which Christianity exists to those who place heavy loads on others' shoulders without lifting a finger to help (23:4), who parade their piety in public for the praise of others (vv. 5–7), or who revel in the exalted titles by which they are addressed (vv. 8–10), and so on. Here appear crucial activities to avoid lest we be found fighting against God himself.[28]

Apocalyptic Discourse

Matthew 24–25 introduces us to the one major example in the Gospels of apocalyptic literature—a literary genre known from the Old Testament as well as intertestamental Jewish and Greco-Roman literature. Its major appearance in the New Testament comes with the Book of Revelation, which I discuss at the end of this chapter. Here, however, we may briefly remark that apocalyptic discourse typically depicts past, present, and especially fu-

ture events in highly symbolic garb—not to enable one to predict
in advance when and how the prophecies will be fulfilled (at least
not in any detail), but rather to encourage God's people in unusually bleak times that he remains in charge and that he is bringing
human history to defined goals, which ultimately include rescue
and deliverance of his people, at least spiritually if not physically.[29] Jesus' apocalyptic (or eschatological) discourse in fact is
designed to temper an "end-times" enthusiasm that thinks it can
discern from current events that we are living in the last generation of human history. The "signs" that Jesus supplies for his disciples are events that should *not* alarm them, because "these
things must happen, but the end is still to come" (or "not yet"—
Matt. 24:6 par.).[30] While interpreters debate which part of Jesus'
message answers the disciples' question about the destruction of
the temple in their day and which part addresses their question
about his return (v. 3), almost everyone agrees that the point of
Jesus' message was to encourage faithful, godly living no matter
how long or short the future turned out to be (thus Matt.
24:43–25:46). Sadly, each century of church history has had those
who altogether missed this central application, preferring instead
to speculate as to when and in whom the end-time events would
be fulfilled. To date, a full 100 percent of these speculations have
proved false, which should inspire considerable humility on the
part of those who would keep on guessing![31]

Passion Narratives

The accounts of Jesus' last night with his disciples, his arrest, trials, and crucifixion (Matthew 26–27 par.) form what are often
called the Passion narratives. The most basic issue in applying
these texts is distinguishing between what was unique to Jesus'
context and what was exemplary for all believers. Obviously, only
Christ's death atoned for the sins of the world. And, because
Christ knew in advance it was God's plan for him to be crucified,
he also knew he should not fight back in the garden (26:52–54) or
defend himself in court (v. 62). We may not automatically take
these behaviors as illustrative of a pacifism required of all believers everywhere. In fact, Jesus himself promised the disciples
would speak and bear testimony when brought to trial for their
faith (10:19–20). But all disciples can expect some kinds of perse-

cutions and hardships as believers, and some will lay down their lives as martyrs (16:24–27). Here is the abiding application of the Passion narratives for believers, which again gives the lie to the so-called health-wealth or prosperity gospel.

Paradigmatic Patterns

A special category of symbolic action finds two examples in Jesus' Passion narrative. Twice Jesus illustrates profound theological truth through his dramatic object lessons and then calls his disciples to imitate him. The event that almost all branches of Christianity have recognized as a "sacrament" or "ordinance" to be repeated wherever the church gathers is Jesus' Last Supper (26:17–30 par.). Christians apply this passage as they share bread and wine, reflect on how it represents the broken body and shed blood of Christ, and thus celebrate what has come to be called "the Lord's Supper," "Holy Communion," or "the Eucharist."[32] In John's Gospel, however, instead of the "Words of Institution" that explain the new meaning Jesus invests into the Passover bread and wine, Jesus washes the disciples' feet and commands his followers to do likewise (John 13:2–17). While a few branches of the church have literally repeated this ceremony in the context of worship on a regular basis, most recognize the practice to be a paradigm of the lifestyle of humble service believers should emulate.[33]

Resurrection Narratives

A subcategory of miracle stories, the resurrection narratives do not explicitly spell out their application with calls to recognize who Jesus is and to follow him, as appear elsewhere in the accounts of Jesus' miracles. But this response is clearly appropriate. One of the most enigmatic passages in all the Gospels, however, may in fact point to a second, central application. In Matthew 27:51–53, a small group of "saints" is resurrected along with Jesus, coming out of their tombs after Christ's resurrection and appearing to many.[34] Numerous questions about this account remain unanswerable (who were they? who saw them? how long did they continue to appear? etc.). But at least one point may be made with some confidence. In light of the Jewish conviction that all people would one day be raised, some to everlasting life and some to eternal punishment (see esp. Dan. 12:2), Matthew seems to be implying by his inclusion of this passage that Jesus' resurrection is the "firstfruit" of the coming general resurrection of all people, a few of whom were likewise raised with Jesus in anticipation of many more to come. Paul, of course, will make this point more explicit in 1 Corinthians 15:23.

Johannine Discourses and Dialogues

Mark and Luke largely parallel Matthew with respect to the literary forms in which they couch Jesus' teachings and actions. John, on the other hand, includes numerous more lengthy discourses and dialogues of Jesus with various audiences. These may in turn be divided into several subcategories.

First, Jesus engages in lengthy *dialogues with individuals.* John 3 and 4 are largely devoted to presenting the back-to-back conversations Jesus has with Nicodemus and the Samaritan woman. These two individuals contrast with each other in just about every way imaginable, including gender, religion, ethnicity, access to education, morality, honor, and power. Yet Nicodemus's contributions to his conversation become progressively shorter and demonstrate his growing perplexity, while the Samaritan woman holds her own as an equal conversation partner with Jesus, responds with faith, and becomes an evangelist to her own people. The juxtaposition of these two characters in consecutive chapters makes the contrast between the two characters that much more striking and suggests that John's main point is to surprise his readers with who turns out to believe and who does not. As with the theme of the "great reversal" in the Synoptics, we are invited to consider who are the comparable people in our world and how it is that they defy our expectations concerning who is most likely to believe and who is not.[35]

Second, some of John's more uninterrupted discourses of Jesus demonstrate *chiasmus* (i.e., an inverted parallel structure). John 5:19–30 affords a clear example, as the outline below demonstrates:

Principle of imitation + rationale (vv. 19–20a)   (v. 30)
    Teaching about "marveling" (v. 20b)   (vv. 28–29)
        Illustrations of life/judgment (vv. 21–23)   (vv. 26–27)
            + purpose or reason
                Double-"Amen"
                saying on salvation (v. 24)   (v. 25)[36]

The purpose of a chiasm is to place the climax of the construction at the center rather than the end of the passage. Thus the central idea of this "sermon" appears in verses 24–25, with Jesus' repeated emphasis that those who hear his word and believe will live eternally. Interpretation and hence application should focus on this "big idea." Those who trust in Christ can experience a different quality of life now in this world (v. 24) as well as in the world to come (v. 25). Is that our vision for the Christian life and for our churches' lives?

Jesus' entire Farewell Discourse (John 14–16) seems likewise to be chiastically arranged, even though not every section heading quite as clearly incorporates all of the detail treated under it:

14:1 Introduction: Don't let your hearts be troubled. Trust in God and me.	16:33 Conclusion: You may have peace in me despite trouble from world.
14:2–14 Jesus is going to the Father (prepare a place/he is way/Father in him)	16:17–32 Jesus is going to the Father (grief to joy/ask in his name)
14:15–21 Jesus promises Paraclete (Spirit of truth to be with disciples)	16:5–16 Jesus promises Paraclete (Spirit of truth to convict world and lead disciples into all truth)
14:22–31 Jesus' revelation to disciples and not to world (Spirit's teaching versus prince of darkness)	15:18–16:4 World's hatred and rejection of disciples' testimony (Spirit's enabling of witness)
15:1–8 The Vine and the Branches: Abiding in Jesus/producing much fruit	15:9–17 Loving like Jesus/sacrificial self-giving[37]

If something like this outline is at all on target, then again the most important point appears in the central material of 15:1–17, which certainly proves crucial theologically. Believers must be so attached to Jesus that their lifestyle becomes like his, even to the point of dying for their faith, should it ever come to that. In our Western world of countless professions of Christian commitment accompanied by so little substantive change in behavior, it is worth asking how many believers truly belong to Christ.

A third kind of discourse is well illustrated by Jesus' sermon in the Capernaum synagogue in John 6:25–59. The bulk of this material (vv. 31–58) forms a unity following the Jewish rhetorical and literary form known as a *proem midrash*.[38] A text of Scripture is introduced for discussion (v. 31), which is then exegeted and paraphrased (vv. 32–40). Certain elements of this discussion lead to a second, related Scripture (vv. 41–44), which is then expounded (vv. 45–47). Finally, attention returns to the first passage with further exposition (vv. 48–58). The theme that unites this material here is the scriptural allusion to "bread from heaven."[39] Audaciously, Jesus is claiming to be the Bread of Life himself, providing spiritual nourishment for God's people, just as Yahweh had provided literal bread in the wilderness (the manna) during the Israelites' wanderings in Moses' day. Applications should thus focus on this central Scripture and Jesus' claim to have fulfilled it. Spiritual nurture takes precedence over physical nurture for believers, and only in Christ is such sustenance truly available.

A fourth category of Johannine discourse finds Jesus in *dialogue with the crowds*. John 7:14–52 discloses a characteristic effect of this form of discourse, illustrated in the Synoptics by Jesus' speaking in parables (Mark 4:10–12 par.), namely, the polarization of Christ's audience (see esp. John 7:40–52). While the New Testament presents numerous diverse models for evangelism, sooner or later our presentation of the gospel must be clear and pointed enough that it calls for a decision. When this happens, if we have adequately re-presented the message, some will be drawn to become believers and others will be repelled. If we never experience a response other than neutrality or indifference, we probably have not adequately explained what is at stake!

John 8:31–59 offers a second example of Jesus in dialogue with the crowds, vividly illustrating one prong of this polarized response. Those who had appeared actually to believe in Jesus early in the dialogue (vv. 30–31) are among those attempting to stone him by the end of the chapter (v. 59). They perceive only blasphemy when Jesus refers to himself with the divine name of Exodus 3:14 (v. 58—"before Abraham was born, *I am*" [italics mine]). Methodologically, this passage illustrates several key principles involved in applying the Johannine discourses and dialogues. In almost every one of them a central christological claim appears, often couched in the form of an "I am" statement—Jesus claiming to be the Bread of Life, Living Water, Resurrection and Life, and so on. Whatever other teaching each passage contains, obedience is not complete unless one acknowledges Jesus as who he claims to be—the incarnation of God himself.

Moreover, it is not initial profession of belief but "remaining" in him that counts (from Gk. *menō*—a verb the KJV regularly translated as "abide"). Paradoxically, John's Gospel has some of the strongest affirmations in the New Testament of the security of the believer (e.g., John 6:39–40; 10:29), while insisting that those who do not remain in Christ will be "cut off" (15:2). John apparently believes that only as one looks back on a person's life and sees if he or she remained in or departed from the faith can one determine who was a genuine believer (1 John 2:19). Security comes as one continues—present tense—to believe (1 John 5:13).[40] And the Johannine discourses of Jesus dialoguing with the crowds and Jewish authorities provide some of the clearest New Testament illustrations of this principle.

Finally, as Jesus nears the end of his life, John portrays him in *extended exhortation of his disciples.* Almost all of the principles needed to apply these messages have already emerged in other Gospel teaching on discipleship. But one unique feature appears in 17:20–23. This is the only place in the Gospels where Jesus directly refers to us who live in the twenty-first century! For that matter, he refers to all believers in the postapostolic era, as he prays not merely for the disciples present with him but "also for those who will believe in me through their message" (v. 20). Everyone who has come to faith after the death of the Twelve has done so because of either the oral or written Word that has preserved first-century truths. Thus it should be quite important to see what Jesus prayed for this community of his followers down through the centuries. Tellingly, he prays for their unity, a oneness that in some sense resembles the unity he has with his Father, and this so that "the world will know" that Christ was truly heaven-sent (v. 23). While a handful of major divides in the history of the church have no doubt been required to preserve fundamental, core Christian doctrine, God cannot possibly be pleased

with the thousands of church splits that have occurred throughout history and around the world over far more trivial matters.
Genuine, born-again believers must ask themselves again and
again how they can better partner in unity with one another so
that unbelievers will want to share in that unique, God-generated
love.[41]

The Acts of the Apostles

Many of the difficulties in deciding what to do with the events in
the Book of Acts stem from *their transitional nature*. With the crucifixion, resurrection, and ascension of Jesus and God's sending of
the Spirit at Pentecost, we encounter the shift from the "Old Testament age" to the "New Testament era." What was perfectly appropriate, perhaps even mandated for God's people, frequently
changes during the transition from old to new. The first generation of Christians comes to believe that they no longer need to
offer animal sacrifices, because Christ is the once-for-all sacrifice
for the forgiveness of sins. "Through him everyone who believes
is set free from every sin, a justification you were not able to ob-
tain under the law of Moses" (Acts 13:39). The dietary laws are rescinded (chap. 10), and there is no longer one uniquely holy land
or temple (chap. 7) as the ideal place where God's people must
worship him. But the first Christians do not wake up the morning
after Pentecost and recognize every one of these changes instantly. The transitions come gradually, which means that applications of Acts cannot simply assume that every apostolic action
is meant to be imitated.

Thus we may not necessarily infer that Paul's purification and
payment for certain Jewish Christians' animal sacrifices was a
good idea, much less God's will, especially when the plan desired
to rebuild trust among Paul's critics disastrously backfires (22:20–
36). Even more tellingly, the apostles' casting of lots (a sort of
rolling of the sacred dice) to determine Judas's replacement (Acts
1:26) follows established Old Testament precedent but never
again appears in the New Testament. The coming of the Holy
Spirit, to permanently indwell believers at Pentecost, provides a
kind of guidance unavailable in many Old Testament settings and
renders lot-casting obsolete.[42]

In addition to paying careful attention to where a practice appears in the development of the church's understanding of the new covenant, several other principles aid us in applying Acts. A key, second step is to look for *Luke's narrative clues.* When no direct command is given to believers, it is easy to wonder whether a given story offers models to imitate or to avoid. The early Christian communal sharing in Acts 2:42–47 and 4:32–5:11 has been cited, on the one hand, as an exemplary model and a reason for supporting modern-day communism, and, on the other hand, as a failed experiment and a practice to avoid! Both perspectives go beyond what the text explicitly supports, but it is telling that Luke describes the results of the practice as care for the poor, joy, praise for God, high regard for the apostles, miraculous healings, and additional people being saved (2:46–47; 5:12–16). The judgment of Ananias and Sapphira (5:1–11), the one strikingly negative result, came not because they either did or did not participate in sharing their possessions, but because they lied about the extent to which they were participating (vv. 2–4). So it is best to conclude that the pictures of communal sharing are positive examples to imitate.[43]

But that raises another question that leads to a third principle for applying Acts. How slavishly must we mimic their model? When Acts offers us exemplary narratives, we must next ask *how consistently does Acts itself reproduce the model?*[44] In the case of meeting the needs of the poor, there are three key paradigms, all presented as helpful, but each quite different from the next. In Acts 6:1–7, precedent for the later office of "deacon" is established—certain leaders are chosen to supervise a daily distribution of food or money for the poor. No longer do the apostles administer a common treasury of funds. Then in 11:27–30 a special offering is taken to meet the needs of Christians suffering the most severely during a time of famine. Three different models all prove effective in different circumstances, but the common thread is material provision for the poor. This suggests that contemporary application could follow any one of these three models, or invent others, so long as Christians with surplus material possessions still share generously with their needier brothers and sisters.[45]

In other instances, a particular model remains unchanged throughout the book. When the Philippian jailer asks Paul and Silas what he must do to be right with God, they reply, "Believe in the Lord Jesus, and you will be saved" (Acts 16:31). This is the consistent means of salvation throughout Acts. In fact, 4:12 generalizes, declaring, "Salvation is found in no one else, for there is no other name given under heaven by which we must be saved." We are safe in concluding that Luke, like Paul, believed that salvation comes solely through belief in Jesus.

In some cases, it is difficult to determine if Acts presents an inviolate pattern or diverse models. What about the coming of the Holy Spirit into a person's life? Acts 2:38–39 seems clearly to present a universal norm: "Repent and be baptized, every one of you, in the name of Jesus Christ for the forgiveness of your sins. And you will receive the gift of the Holy Spirit. The promise is for you and your children and for all who are far off—for all whom the Lord our God will call." And the *normal* pattern in the rest of the book is that whenever someone truly believes, the Holy Spirit indwells them and empowers them for Christian obedience. What, then, do we do with the one apparently glaring exception to this pattern—the Samaritans who respond to Philip's preaching with apparent belief but who do not receive the Spirit until Peter and John come down from Jerusalem to lay hands on them (8:12–17)?[46]

Some have tried to make this exception the norm and insist on a "second blessing" of the Spirit's power *subsequent* to conversion, but exceptions make bad case law! Others have argued that there is *no* normative pattern, but this overlooks the general trend in Acts itself as well as Paul's firm assertion in Romans 8:9 that "if anyone does not have the Spirit of Christ, they do not belong to Christ." Probably the most common approach taken by evangelical commentators is that this was an exceptional approach for an exceptional situation. Because it represented the first widespread conversion of Samaritans to Christianity, it was by no means assured that the exclusively Jewish Christian community would welcome these former enemies on equal terms within the fledgling church. Perhaps the apostolic leaders needed to confirm for themselves the legitimacy of these new conversions. What better way than for the Holy Spirit to manifest himself in a tangible way precisely through the ministry of Peter and John?

On the other hand, it may be that this passage is not the exception that it seems to be. Simon the Magician is also said to have believed (v. 13) but quickly demonstrates that his "heart is not right before God" (v. 21), to such a degree that Peter pronounces a curse on him (v. 20). Maybe the "belief" of the other Samaritans is likewise only apparent, and it is only after Peter and John come and instruct them further that they truly understand and are saved.[47] Whether or not this passage is truly an exception within the Book of Acts, the important point for applying this text is that it cannot be turned into a requirement that all believers must have some extra, subsequent, dramatic empowering of the Holy Spirit after their initial salvation in order for their Christian life to be mature. On the other hand, no text of Scripture ever excludes the possibility that the Spirit may at certain times, in his sovereignty, choose to bless *some* of Christ's followers in special ways as he did the Samaritans.

A fourth key principle in applying Acts involves *contextualization*—couching the gospel in language that best communicates its essence in a specific context.[48] Perhaps the main reason one so often has to look throughout the whole book to determine which models prove consistent and which ones vary is because the first Christians worked hard to incarnate the gospel in the diverse cultures in which they ministered. The sermons in Acts afford a classic example. On the one hand, there are common elements in almost all of them, irrespective of who the preacher is—an appeal to general or special revelation to establish common ground with the audience, references to Jesus as the fulfillment of all previous religious aspirations, a focus on his death and resurrection as the heart of the Christian message, and an appeal to repent or to become Christ's followers.[49] On the other hand, no two messages are identical. Paul, whose sermons occupy the largest percentage of speeches in Acts, carefully tailors each message to its context. To Jews in the synagogue, he appeals to Old Testament history and to numerous Scriptures that he believes point to Christ (13:16–41). To pagans in Lystra, he stresses God's testimony through nature (14:15–18). To philosophically minded Athenians, he appeals to an unknown God to whom they have erected an altar, quotes Greek poetry, and plays Stoic and Epicurean philosophies against one another (17:22–31). And to the elders from the churches in and around Ephesus, he sounds most like the Paul of the Epistles—talking about the centrality of God's grace, faith in Jesus, his atoning blood, and the danger of false teachers (20:17–35). This is not surprising, since all of Paul's letters are likewise addressed to *Christian* audiences.[50]

Unfortunately, at many points in church history, Christians have not carefully balanced these twin features of a common core message and careful contextualization. Either they create a "one-size-fits-all" program of evangelism that does not address distinctive backgrounds, understandings, and needs of each individual person or audience, or they work so hard to relate to each distinctive setting that fundamental material is left out. Kenneth Gangel's words from a generation ago remain as true today as when they were first written:

> The intelligentsia of American society today have not been offered by contemporary Christianity as distinctive a witness to truth as that heard by the Greek philosophers in Athens on that day. The "preaching of the cross" does not have to consist of simplistic verbal meanderings calculated to evoke appropriate emotional responses. The Areopagus sermon offers us a standard of excellence in depth and relevance. Let the modern day Athenians hear again the word of the Risen Christ.[51]

A fifth principle for applying Acts is to *stress what Luke devotes the most space to in his narration.* When one is not primarily giving commands but recounting history, a common device for highlighting the most crucial material involves the use of narrative space. Stories that are told in more detail or in a more leisurely manner are usually more important. Or the narrator may refer back to the same event more than once. Thus, while it is scarcely the most well-known speech in Acts, Stephen's "defense" before the Sanhedrin (7:2–53) is narrated in the greatest detail. Given the freedom ancient historians felt to abbreviate their accounts, Luke must see something of great importance here. Stephen may well have been the first Christian to recognize the extent to which Christ's coming brought freedom from the Jewish Law, a key emphasis throughout the speech. That freedom proved crucial to the development of Christianity from an exclusively Jewish sect into a major worldwide religion for all peoples.[52] Wherever freedom in Christ does not remain central in contemporary Christian experience, Acts in general and Stephen's speech in particular need to be applied liberally!

Peter's encounter with Cornelius affords an excellent example of emphasis by repetition. Not only does Luke relate the episode in minute detail (chap. 10), he takes another large chunk of text to have Peter retell his story all over again to the church leaders in Jerusalem (11:1–18). He then describes how Peter referred back to this incident again at the Apostolic Council (15:6–11).[53] Clearly the breakthrough often known as the "Gentile Pentecost" was crucial for Luke's understanding of the growth of Christianity. Not only was the church freed from the Law of Moses, the gospel was available for Gentiles on the identical terms as for Jews.

A final principle is the flip side of the last one. Often more minor details in lengthy narratives are present simply because they better help us understand the central points, move the story along to its next scene, or add artistry or aesthetic delight to the account. One needs to be careful, therefore, and *not ascribe too much significance to the more peripheral details of narratives.* The best example in Acts is the lengthy description of Paul's ill-fated voyage to Rome and the shipwreck that ensued. The numerous ports of call and the rich, nautical detail in chapter 27 add historical credibility as well as a sense of suspense and adventure to the account.[54] The severity of the storm and the extent of the danger magnify God's grace in sparing the lives of all on board. But we should not attempt to find personal applications for believers today from the details of the direction of the wind, the passing of the island called Cauda, the securing of the lifeboats, the fear of sandbars, the lowering of anchors, and so on (vv. 13–20). Applications must come rather from such theological portions of the passage as the encouragement for the sailors and God's promises to Paul (vv. 21–26).

The Epistles of Paul

NORMATIVE OR SITUATION-SPECIFIC?

Undoubtedly, the biggest difficulty in applying the Epistles is the question of when specific commands are timeless in nature and when they apply only under certain circumstances. We must never lose sight of the "occasional" nature of the New Testament letters, especially Paul's, inasmuch as all of his letters were initially addressed to *one* Christian congregation or individual.[55]

While no list can ever cover every possibility, the following series of questions can go a long way in determining how broadly epistolary instructions were meant to be applied.

First, *does the immediate context juxtapose a seemingly contradictory command?* If so, then probably each part of the passage contains implicit limitations on its application. Romans 12:17–21 has been taken as support for full-fledged pacifism: "Do not repay anyone evil for evil . . . live at peace with everyone. Do not take revenge. . . . If your enemy is hungry, feed him; if he is thirsty, give him something to drink. . . . Do not be overcome by evil, but overcome evil with good." Yet 13:1–7 immediately turns to the responsibility to be subject to governing authorities, who "do not bear the sword for no reason. They are God's servants, agents of wrath to bring punishment on the wrongdoer" (v. 4). Even without any belief in the Bible's inspiration, one usually grants otherwise coherent, intelligent writers the benefit of the doubt that they do not flatly contradict themselves in short compass. Presumably, 12:17–21 refers to the distinctively Christian reaction of believers and churches to their enemies, while 13:1–7 outlines the responsibility of governments.[56]

Second, *does the command seem to contradict teaching elsewhere in Paul's writings?* Again, it may be that one or both of the passages in which the apparent tension is perceived are being applied too widely. Thus, while 1 Corinthians 14:33–38 does not come immediately after 11:2–16, it is again reasonable to assume that the first text helps to qualify the second.[57] In 11:5, Paul tacitly approves of women praying or prophesying so long as they have the appropriate head-covering on. When he then declares three chapters later that "women should remain silent in the churches" (14:34), it is likely that he has some specific kind of speech in mind. Without going into the complex debate, the two most probable kinds of speaking in view are the evaluation of prophecy (a task ultimately falling to the leadership of the church and the topic most recently discussed in the context of this verse) and distracting interruptions based on a lack of previous education (which would explain why the women should ask their own husbands at home—v. 35). It is possible even to combine these two views. In either event, the passage should not be applied today so as to silence women in all church settings![58]

Third, *does the rationale for a specific command work equally well in all cultures?* If not, again, there may be situation-specific dimensions present. Returning to 1 Corinthians 11, it is debated whether Paul has external head-coverings or simply hair in mind in verses 4–10, as well as if he is drawing on his Jewish background or on the Corinthians' Greco-Roman culture. In every known combination of factors, however, uncovered heads or short hair on women and covered heads or long hair on men suggested religious and/or sexual infidelity. In cultures where this symbolism is absent, faithful application of Paul's commands means *not* literally worrying about head-coverings but asking what cultural equivalents *do* send the same misleading signals. In the Western world, these might include a married person refusing to wear a wedding ring or publicly flirting; along with any believer, single or married, wearing overly suggestive clothing or dressing too much like a worshiper in some non-Christian religion.[59]

In verses 14–16, however, it is clear that Paul *is* speaking about short and long hair. Here the reasons he gives for claiming that long hair on a man is a "disgrace" (v. 14) while on a woman "it is her glory" (v. 15) at first glance appear to be more timeless—"the very nature of things" (v. 14) and the practice of all the churches (v. 16). Yet Paul's Jewish upbringing would have taught him about at least one category of uniquely consecrated man who *never* cut his hair—the Nazirite (see esp. Numbers 6)—so "the nature of things" must here refer to first-century Greco-Roman customs. So, too, the practice of all the churches cannot mean anything more than "during the first century," even if Paul's instruction here was meant for all of his congregations.[60]

First Corinthians 11 obviously demonstrates the need for us to do a little historical homework and to understand the factors at work in the first century when the Epistles were written. At the same time, application can appeal to unstated historical background too quickly and miss the clear statement of the text itself. For example, 1 Corinthians 7:25–28 expresses Paul's preference for the single life. Because comparatively few people throughout church history have shared this preference, it is natural to look for some contextually limiting factor that influenced Paul. Some commentators have recalled the famine during the late 40s and suggest that lingering effects are making life in Corinth unusually difficult. Thus the "present crisis" in verse 26 that makes life for married people full of troubles (v. 28) becomes something that other Christians in other times and places do not face. Those Christians, then, should eagerly seek to marry, or so the argument goes.

But verses 29–35 go on in considerable detail to itemize what Paul means by the present crisis—"the time is short" (v. 29), "this world in its present form is passing away" (v. 31), and a married person's concerns are more divided than a single person's (vv. 32–35). The first two of these rationales reflect Paul's awareness that the world could end at any time. The third is clearly cross-cultural. All three reasons therefore remain timeless. The time is even shorter now than it was in Paul's day, while married persons' interests are still divided. Christians like John Stott and Lottie Moon have consciously opted to remain single to serve the Lord with greater, undivided devotion, and all believers should at least seriously consider this option. Paul makes it clear throughout chapter 7 that he is not absolutizing this perspective (vv. 9, 28a, 36, 38a, 39), but how many Christians have ever even raised the question?[61]

Fourth, *does a command appeal to the way God first established things in Old Testament times or to the way he is reestablishing them in New Testament times?* If so, the instruction probably contains a timeless dimension, which also reflects the restoration of some original pattern that had been abandoned. The most important example from Paul's letters is his repeated argument that faith predated the Law. Because Abraham was justified by faith more than four hundred years before the Law was introduced (and because he was justified by faith in his own life before his classic "good work" of preparing to sacrifice his son Isaac), faith takes priority over the commandments of Moses (Romans 4; Gal. 3:1–18). Applications of these themes from Paul's letters should confront legalism, nomism, and ethnocentrism in our world—the triad of first-century manifestations of an inappropriate emphasis on the works of the Law—and seek to replace them with salvation by grace through faith alone.[62]

More controversial are the examples of what have been called "creation ordinances." Few balk, in the Gospels, when Jesus argues for monogamous marriage for life on the basis of the way God created Adam and Eve, before his concessions to divorce in the Mosaic Law, and even before the Fall corrupted humanity at all (Matt. 19:1–12 par.). But when Paul appeals to the order of creation to support his prohibition of women teaching or exercising authority over men in church, the debates rage (1 Tim. 2:13). Of course, a complicating factor involves the difficulty of translating key words and phrases in Paul's prohibition in verse 12. I have elsewhere argued that Paul is not prohibiting two unrelated actions (teaching and exercising authority) but the role of "authoritative teaching," which 1 Timothy subsequently equates with the distinctive role of an elder or overseer (3:1–7; 5:17). But it is hard to escape the conclusion that, however one understands Paul's prohibition, he intended it to be timeless.[63]

This conclusion is reinforced by the logic of his instructions for husbands and wives in Ephesians 5:22–27. It is possible to argue that grounding a command in the Old Testament era before the Law still reflects a period of time corrupted by the Fall. It is even possible to claim that a creation ordinance may not be entirely cross-cultural, since the conditions of new creation in Christ at times go beyond the original creation. Witness how Christ's incarnation represents a permanent addition of a human nature to the divine nature he had from all eternity past. Yet Paul can command both a wife's submission and a husband's sacrificial love by a direct analogy with Christ. The woman's submission must be "as to the Lord," the man's headship mirrors Christ's authority over the church, and his love must model Jesus' self-giving. Unless it is the case that "the church submits to Christ" only in certain times and places (v. 24a), it cannot be that "wives should submit to their husbands" (v. 24b) only in certain cultures. Unless Christ loved and gave himself up only for some people in some cultures (v. 25b), it cannot be that husbands are to love their wives sacrificially only in certain times and places (v. 25a)![64]

Fifth, *does a command reflect a broad cross-cultural principle stated explicitly in the text?* If so, we may expect it to be timeless. When Paul insists that only through faith in Christ may people become right with God, his rationale is that "all have sinned and fall short of the glory of God" (Rom. 3:23). From Romans 1:18–3:20, it is clear that "all" means every human being without exception, since Paul first makes the point with respect to all Gentiles (1:18–32), then refers to all the Jews (2:1–3:8), and, finally, via ten Old Testament quotations, reinforces the generalization that no one, Jew or Gentile, is righteous, not even one (3:9–20).[65]

On the other hand, in other passages what at first appears to be a sweeping generalization may turn out to be more narrowly focused, especially when one observes the larger context in which it is embedded. Romans 14:14 literally reads, "I know and am persuaded in the Lord Jesus that nothing is unclean in itself." This text has been abused over the centuries by some to justify various kinds of immorality, but if one reads the entire chapter it becomes clear that Paul is talking about debates over clean and unclean *food*. In an era when some Jewish Christians still insisted on keeping the old dietary laws, Paul insists that no food is inherently impure (as in fact some English translations spell out).[66]

Sixth, especially when one of Paul's letters is addressed to an individual rather than a church, we must ask *what is uniquely applicable to that individual rather than being required of all believers?* For example, in 1 Timothy 4:11–16, Paul gives a series of commands to Timothy in his role as pastor of the Ephesian church. Most of them can apply to Christians who are not church leaders, too, but verse 13 is clearly more limited: "Until I come, devote yourself to the public reading of Scripture, to preaching and to teaching." Other pastors should apply this command to their "job descriptions" as well, but Paul did not imagine all Christians performing these three tasks.

Other Principles

Here I can present only some of the most important concepts with brief illustrations. I will enumerate seven additional principles for applying Paul's letters.

First, *determine where the emphasis in a passage is placed, especially if there seem to be competing principles within it.* In 1 Corinthians 8:1–11:1, Paul discusses food sacrificed to idols and other morally neutral matters. On the one hand, chapter 8 stresses that believers should take care not to lead other Christians into actual sin (or into sinning against their own conscience by engaging in something they do not feel free to do). On the other hand, 9:19–23 emphasizes that believers are inherently free to make their own choices in these gray areas. In fact, when it is an issue of relating to unbelievers, they should avoid any potentially legalistic restrictions on their behavior that could place unnecessary obstacles in the paths of those who still need to come to faith. At the end of this section, Paul repeats both points, but in sandwich fashion:

first freedom (10:25–27); then voluntary restraint (vv. 28–29a); then freedom again (vv. 29b–30). The same a-b-a pattern, with the same elements, appears in Romans 14:1–12, 14:13–15:4, and 15:7–13. Freedom is the main point; restraint, the lesser one. So if one has to choose between stressing the freedom of the gospel and emphasizing restrictions in morally neutral areas, one should choose freedom—a lesson that countless legalists in the history of the church have never learned![67]

Second, *specific applications may often be applied to analogous situations that are otherwise never addressed in Scripture.* The example of food sacrificed to idols again affords a classic example. A long catalog of analogous issues may prove more relevant in other times and places, including the temperate use of alcohol, forms of recreation and dress, styles of music, and so on.[68] Or to consider a quite different example, there is nothing in the Bible about being "slain in the Spirit"—when a person physically falls down and at times writhes around in response to some kind of "charismatic" activity. But Paul does address the somewhat similar supernatural phenomenon of tongues throughout 1 Corinthians 14. Presumably the same principles apply to both situations, summed up in Paul's concluding call not to forbid the exercise of the gift but to use it "in a fitting and orderly way" (i.e., in ways that build up rather than divide the community)—verses 39–40.[69]

Third, *note what would have stood out in Paul's world as cutting against the grain of his society or culture.* These are probably the practices Paul is most emphasizing. Ancient Jewish, Greek, and Roman literature regularly addressed the responsibilities of people in relationships of authority and subordination. The literary form of commands to these various groups of persons has come to be known as a "domestic code." Little of what Paul said to wives in his codes would have seemed countercultural, but the command for husbands to engage in self-giving sacrificial love would have shocked many (cf. esp. Eph. 5:22–24 with vv. 25–28).[70] Undoubtedly this is where emphasis should still be placed today, though few Christians seem to recognize this. Likewise, Paul's principles concerning sacrificial financial giving (see esp. 2 Corinthians 8–9) would have seemed foolish to Jews, who forbade giving away more than 20 percent of one's income, and to Gentiles, who did not even have any empire-wide system for meeting the needs of their poor as the Jews did. Practicing a graduated tithe remains countercultural today but is arguably what faithful application of Paul's teaching requires.[71]

Fourth, *distinguish between what uniquely applies to God or Jesus and what can be imitated by all Christians.* Philippians 2:5–11 depicts Christ's incarnation, crucifixion, resurrection, and exaltation. Paul inserts this hymn where he does because he wants Christians in their relationships with one another to "have the same attitude of mind Christ Jesus had" (v. 5). But none of us is fully divine as well as fully human, so our imitation can be only partial. We cannot decide to forego using selfishly our "equality with God" (v. 6), because we possess no such equality. Nor can we look forward to being "exalted to the highest place" (v. 9), once again at the right hand of the Father. But we can refuse to turn the privileges of the Christian life into something to be used to our own advantage, and we can endure injustice in this life better when we recognize the glorious resurrection life that one day awaits us.[72]

Fifth, *try to discern the overall structure of an epistle.* Often main points of application will emerge from the "big ideas" of main divisions of the letter. Also the sequence of topics may yield important insights regarding application. Philippians has been convincingly outlined as a "family" or "friendship" letter:

Greetings and Thanksgiving (1:1–11)
Reassurance about the Sender: Description of Paul's Imprisonment (1:12–26)
Request for Reassurance about the Recipients: Call to Christlike Living (1:27–2:18)
Information about Movement of Intermediaries: Concerning Timothy and Epaphroditus (2:19–30)
Special Concern: Warnings about the False Teachers (3:1–4:1)
Final Instructions, Thank-Yous, and Greetings (4:2–23)[73]

The two sections warning against Judaizers and thanking the Philippians for money sent diverge from the standard pattern and demonstrate the immediate reasons for Paul's writings. But one main application can be derived from each section of the body of the letter as it stands: (1) Encourage others about your well-being in ministry; (2) challenge others to the unity that comes from treating others as more important than self; (3) commend faithful believers publicly; (4) warn against heresy forthrightly, when in fact people's salvation is at stake, but only then; (5) thank people for their support and be content however little or great it is.

In the case of the exhortational portion of Romans (12:1–15:13), it is the sequence of subsections that seems significant. First, Paul commands all believers to be transformed in body and mind (12:1–2). Then he instructs each to discover and utilize his or her spiritual gift(s) (vv. 3–8). What seems at first glance to be a more miscellaneous set of commands (12:9–13:14) is actually set in the framework of injunctions to love (12:9–13; 13:8–14); the intervening material, particularly on dealing with one's enemies, certainly illustrates love. Finally, Paul discusses Christian tolerance more generally (14:1–15:13). When one observes that 1 Corinthians 12–14 exhibits a similar structure—foundational transformation (12:1–3); use of gifts with diversity in unity (12:4–31); love (13:1–13); and mutual tolerance, balancing freedom and restraint (14:1–40)—one suspects that Paul's sequence is deliberate. If one truly wants to know God's will for one's life (Rom. 12:2), one will commit oneself wholly to the Lord, exercise spiritual gifts, in love, while tolerating others whose gifts may be quite different. And it makes sense to do these things in this order.[74]

Sixth, *distinguish the central from the peripheral.* This principle is inherent in some of the guidelines and illustrations I have already given, but it is worth articulating explicitly. One of the striking contrasts in Paul's letters is between the severity with which he condemns false teachers whose beliefs strike at the heart of the gospel and the tolerance with which he allows people to disagree with him on peripheral matters (cf. Gal. 1:6–10 with 1 Cor. 9:19–23).[75] Closely related is the contrast in Philippians between Paul's rejoicing over the preaching of the gospel by rival teachers with improper motives (Phil. 1:15–18) and his anathemas for the Judaizers who pervert the gospel into one of works righteousness (3:2–11). Apparently the former, who preach out of "selfish ambition," still get the core message right, whereas the latter, however well-intentioned, do not. Sadly, today the church often inverts these priorities, either tolerating major heresy (particularly in liberal circles) or warring over unessential matters (particularly in conservative circles). Both behaviors work against Paul's central goal of winning as many to the Lord as possible, through the preaching of the true gospel of Jesus Christ.

Finally, *recognize when Paul lays down principles which could not be fully implemented in his world but which challenge later Christians to move even further in the directions he was already heading.* The classic example here involves slavery. The little letter to Philemon seems to be a request for Philemon to free his slave Onesimus, who has come to Christ through Paul's ministry. First Corinthians 7:21 is difficult to translate but probably teaches that slaves who can gain their freedom should do so. But in Colossians 3:22–25, Paul still calls slaves to submit to their masters (cf. Eph. 6:5–8). Christianity would eventually work to abolish slavery in several societies in different centuries, but there is no evidence that the apostolic church ever began such a movement within the first century. Numerous reasons account for this: its lack of any power base, the varied kinds of slavery in the Roman Empire (many of which were not too severe), the priority of spiritual deliverance over physical liberation, and so on. But it is arguable, with F. F. Bruce, that even the little Paul did teach brings us "into an atmosphere in which the institution could only wilt and die."[76]

Many contemporary writers draw explicit parallels between Paul's teachings on slavery and his instruction on gender roles. After all, Galatians 3:28 clearly pairs the two in declaring, "There is neither Jew nor Greek, neither slave nor free, neither male nor female, for you are all one in Christ Jesus."[77] But parallels to Galatians 3:28 have been discovered in otherwise quite patriarchal writings in ancient Judaism and the Greco-Roman world, so it is difficult to conclude that this verse alone proves that Paul envisioned no remaining role distinctions of any kind for any people as Christians.[78] The issue will have to be settled by detailed analysis of the texts that do appear to preserve fixed roles, such as those already noted throughout this chapter (esp. 1 Cor. 11:2–16; 14:33–38; Eph. 5:22–33; and 1 Tim. 2:8–15).

Hebrews and the General Epistles

All of the principles for valid application of the Pauline epistles work well with the non-Pauline epistles, too, even though several of these books do not conform as closely to the ancient genre of epistle as Paul's letters do.[79] But in several instances, we do not have nearly as much information to enable us to determine the precise date, audience, or even location of the addressees. In most of these instances, however, we can reconstruct in fair detail the circumstances of those who would receive the letters—settings in which the epistle writers felt their audiences needed instruction. One additional approach to applying the epistles, therefore, is to *look for similar settings in our world today.* Application of these comparatively neglected letters will then take on a particular urgency. Space limitations prevent an analysis of every one of these letters, but we will briefly consider three as examples.

Hebrews probably addresses a collection of Jewish Christian house-churches in Rome in the early 60s, as persecution is starting to increase, to encourage believers not to revert back to non-Christian Judaism merely to save their physical lives. The author is unknown, and even these suggestions concerning date, location, and audience are disputed. But it is beyond question that the letter pleads for Christians tempted to commit apostasy by abandoning their faith not to do so, because every other religious option leads only to eternal punishment. Contemporary applications should look for comparable situations where the pressures of government, other religions, or family loyalties tempt professing Christians to renounce their professions. For people who have never literally put their lives on the line for their faith, Hebrews reminds us that we may not fully know people's "true colors" until they face such a crisis.[80]

James's epistle apparently addresses a collection of poor Jewish Christians, probably in Israel or Syria, who worked as day laborers on large agricultural estates, owned by absentee Jewish or Roman landlords who did not always pay them on time or pay enough for them even to feed their families. James's stinging rebuke of these rich oppressors should strike fear in the hearts of their contemporary equivalents—the multinational corporations that fail to pay Third World farmers or factory workers a decent wage, not to mention Westerners, including Christians, who buy their products indiscriminately without trying to determine the conditions under which they were made.[81]

The setting of 1 Peter in many ways resembles that of Hebrews, except that it seems to be written *from* Rome *to* various provinces that today form part of Turkey. Again growing persecution, much of it local, was making life difficult for believers, though here Gentile Christians seem to have predominated. The titles of two important studies of 1 Peter reflect perhaps the two central themes of the book: "a home for the homeless" and "seek the welfare of the city."[82] Far from contradicting each other, these seemingly opposite emphases reflect the inward- and outward-looking responsibilities of the church in every age—providing physical and spiritual refuge from the world and functioning as salt and light in a corrupt society to try to improve it. Particularly in situations with literal refugees today, the principles of 1 Peter cry out to be applied.

The Book of Revelation

As with Jesus' eschatological discourse (see above, pp. 119–20), Revelation represents apocalyptic literature. Application of this literature should not involve trying to correlate current events with the book's highly symbolic imagery, as if Revelation were designed to enable us to recognize as they unfold all the events that will immediately usher in the end of the world. Rather, Revelation 1 should remind us that the book introduces numerous important theological themes—the sovereignty of God, the deity of Christ, the nature of the Trinity, the atonement and the resurrection, and so on (see esp. 1:4–8)—and that even the primary doctrine of eschatology focuses centrally on the *fact* of Christ's return (v. 7), which may be all that Christians can expect (or need) to agree on.[83] The letters to the seven churches (chaps. 2–3) invite us to compare the whole spectrum of faithfulness and faithlessness represented in ancient Asia Minor with analogous churches or branches of Christianity in our world. The same calls to repentance and rewards for obedience apply today. Chapters 4–5 (and scattered other hymns throughout the book) should lead us to praise God for his marvelous works, even as the inhabitants of heaven already do.

Applications of the series of seal, bowl, and trumpet judgments and the interludes that separate them (chaps. 6–19) will vary somewhat, depending on whether the interpreter takes a preterist, historicist, idealist, or futurist approach to the book (or some combination thereof). This debate asks the question, Do these chapters primarily reflect events of the first century (preterist), developments of church history (historicist), timeless principles of the struggle between good and evil (idealist), or still-future events (futurist)? Perhaps the best approach is a primarily futurist one, which nevertheless recognizes partial parallels both in the first century and at other times throughout history, enabling timeless principles to be derived as well.[84] In this light, whether or not any generation turns out actually to be the last one, we may in every age recognize at least the foreshadowings of developments Revelation so graphically depicts. Any anti-Christian world power at least partially resembles the depiction of the end-times Antichrist, but Christians may take heart that God will eventually triumph over every such power.[85] They may undergo severe tribulation, but they are exempt from God's wrath (an affirmation on which pre-, mid-, and post-tribulationists alike agree). They can look forward to eternal rest and bliss, whereas the wicked face only unceasing torment (chaps. 20–22)—a promise with which pre-, post-, and amillennialists all concur. After that, almost every detail varies according to the varying theological systems, but if we are agreed on the essentials we can agree to disagree on the rest.[86]

Conclusion

No mechanical formula exists for properly applying any text of Scripture. The more we understand what a particular passage meant for its original author and audience, the more likely we can understand its original application. The more closely parallel the situation we find ourselves in this day, the more we can simply apply the text in similar fashion. But many times our situations are not terribly comparable. We can still recognize broad principles that transcend time and place, but specific applications may prove more controversial. Understanding the unique issues that attach to the Bible's diverse literary forms enables us to make even more progress toward valid application, but Christians still will disagree on numerous issues.

It is likewise crucial to remember the gracious way in which God's Spirit guides his people. While no one should ever deliberately abuse a text and blame God for guiding them in the process, the Spirit regularly speaks to and through believers even when they *unknowingly* misuse passages, just as the Spirit uses us to accomplish his work in the world even when our motives are less than what they should be. We should thank God that he acts this way. Were it not the case, God would be able to do very little with us, since we so regularly fail to measure up to his standards. But, as in every other area of Christian growth, we should never use God's grace as an excuse for our laziness, or worse (Rom. 6:1). We have more evangelical Christian resources for understanding the Bible in more languages of the world, and especially in English, than ever before in church history. So it is the height of irresponsibility not to avail ourselves of those resources, generated by God-honoring believers who were responding to his call on their lives in producing those tools.[87] At the same time, reading other people's thoughts about the Bible should never supplant our detailed, serious wrestling with the text of Scripture ourselves, prayerfully seeking what God wants to say to us directly in that process.

Summary

Despite numerous claims to the contrary, there are at least a dozen good reasons for believing that the New Testament Gospels and Acts present substantially reliable historical information. Textual criticism allows us to reconstruct what the original authors first wrote with a high degree of confidence. Matthew, Mark, Luke, and John were all in good positions to remember or learn about the life of Jesus. They all wrote their Gospels within the first century, a comparatively short period of time after the events they narrated. The Gospel genre most closely resembles that of other relatively trustworthy ancient biographies and histories. It is probable that the four Evangelists would have wanted to record accurate history, that Christian tradition carefully preserved information about Jesus and the apostles, and that the apparent contradictions among the documents can be plausibly harmonized. This is true, whether we compare the Synoptic Gospels with one another, the Synoptics with John, Acts with Paul's letters, or the New Testament with extrabiblical history more generally. The so-called hard sayings of Jesus, along with the topics the Gospels never address, further support the historicity of these texts. Non-Christian writers, the evidence of archaeology, and later Christian writers all provide further support. Particularly telling are those references to the Jesus tradition in the New Testament epistles that predate the composition of the Gospels. These references demonstrate that accurate information about Jesus was circulating by word of mouth long before the first written accounts of his life were penned.

While at first glance Jesus and Paul may appear to have

stressed very different themes, a closer look finds the two men fundamentally compatible with each other. Paul discloses extensive knowledge of the Jesus tradition, even if he only occasionally quotes Jesus directly. The purpose and genre of the epistles did not lend themselves to extensive direct citation. But numerous allusions appear in Paul's letters to events from Jesus' life, along with a broad cross section of Jesus' individual teachings and larger sermons. A comparison of several central theological components reveals considerable overlap between Jesus and Paul here, too. Paul's emphasis on justification by faith corresponds closely to Jesus' teaching on the kingdom of God. Both men have comparable views on the role of the Law in the Christian era, the need for mission and the inclusion of the Gentiles into the church, and the role of women in ministry. The implicit christology of the Synoptics portrays Jesus having a very high view of himself, making the explicit christology of John and Paul a more natural outgrowth than some have imagined. Both Jesus and Paul recognized the central role of Christ's death, resurrection, and return from heaven. While Paul would have had his thinking transformed in several fundamental ways on the Damascus Road, and can thus attribute the heart of "his gospel" to his conversion experience (Gal. 1:11–12), nothing he says in his letters contradicts the conclusion that he would have learned numerous details about the historical Jesus from fellow Christians.

Applying the New Testament requires, among other things, an understanding of how its diverse literary forms vary. The Gospels were composed primarily to nurture belief in Jesus. They stress his countercultural teaching, compassion for the outcast, and increasing conflicts with the religious authorities of his day. His regular use of metaphors means that we must take care not to interpret literally that which was intended as figurative. The harder or more controversial commands require careful understanding of their historical and literary contexts, as well as distinguishing when Jesus is speaking only to the Twelve or giving other situation-specific commands. One must note his predilection for prophetic object lessons, for apocalyptic discourse, and for extended dialogues or sermons (particularly in John's Gospel), each of which presents the interpreter with distinctive challenges. The key difficulties in applying the Book of Acts stem largely from its narrative form and the transitional period between old and new covenants that it describes. Readers must look for indirect clues that Luke leaves to determine how important or exemplary a given incident is. These clues include the way a passage is introduced or concluded, how often a theme is repeated, whether or not a consistent pattern of behavior emerges across the book, and how much space Luke gives to each topic. The entire book offers a wonderful model for contextualizing the gospel. In the Epistles, the question of what is timeless versus what is situation-specific dominates. Again one must look for apparent contradictions elsewhere, the particular rationales attached to various commands, the possible grounding of a command in creation or new creation, broad cross-cultural principles, and the differences between teaching addressed to all Christians and that which applies only to some. Hebrews and the General Epistles require the use of all these principles, too, but also present new challenges and opportunities for interpreters when they contemporize the circumstances under which these letters were composed. Revelation was not written to enable us to recognize unique signs of the times just preceding Christ's return, but to give hope to God's people in all times and places that he is sovereign, that Jesus wins, and that history is moving toward its appointed goals. In this light, how one responds to Jesus of Nazareth reflects the most important decision anyone can make in this life.

Notes

Introduction

1. Tremper Longman, *Making Sense of the Old Testament: Three Crucial Questions* (Grand Rapids: Baker, 1998).

2. All NT quotations will follow Today's New International Version (TNIV) unless otherwise indicated.

Chapter 1:
Is the New Testament Historically Reliable?

1. James W. Deardorff, *Celestial Teachings: The Emergence of the True Testament of Jmmanuel (Jesus)* (Tigard, Oreg.: Wild Flower Press, 1990) (the "J" is not a typographical error; he spells it that way); idem, *The Problem of New Testament Gospel Origins* (San Francisco: Mellen Research University Press, 1992).

2. William D. Mahan, *The Archko Volume: The Archaeological Writings of the Sanhedrim and Talmuds of the Jews,* ed. M. McIntosh and T. H. Twyman (1887; New Canaan, Conn.: Keats, 1975). The volume continues to be reprinted and widely distributed.

3. See Barbara Thiering, *Jesus and the Riddle of the Dead Sea Scrolls* (San Francisco: HarperSanFrancisco, 1993).

4. See Carsten P. Thiede (*Rekindling the Word: In Search of Gospel Truth* [Valley Forge, Pa.: Trinity Press International, 1995], 37–57, 169–97); and Graham Stanton (*Gospel Truth? New Light on Jesus and the Gospels* [Valley Forge, Pa.: Trinity Press International, 1995], 11–19, 20–32).

5. The *Gospel of Thomas* is the one extracanonical post–New Testament document that some scholars think may contain authentic Jesus tradition separate from the contents of the canonical Gospels. For a survey and negative assessment of these claims and of similar claims held, by far

fewer scholars, concerning other apocryphal Christian literature, see John P. Meier, *A Marginal Jew: Rethinking the Historical Jesus* (New York: Doubleday, 1991–), 1:112–66. See n. 11 below for more on Meier's work.

6. The results are most conveniently accessed in Robert W. Funk, Roy W. Hoover, and the Jesus Seminar, *The Five Gospels: The Search for the Authentic Words of Jesus* (New York: Macmillan, 1993); and Robert W. Funk and the Jesus Seminar, *The Acts of Jesus: The Search for the Authentic Deeds of Jesus* (San Francisco: HarperSanFrancisco, 1998).

7. For a thorough analysis and critique of the Jesus Seminar's methodology and conclusions, see Craig L. Blomberg, "The Seventy-four 'Scholars': Who Does the Jesus Seminar Really Speak For?" *Christian Research Journal* 17, no. 2 (1994): 32–38. More generally, see Michael J. Wilkins and J. P. Moreland, eds., *Jesus Under Fire: Modern Scholarship Reinvents the Historical Jesus* (Grand Rapids: Zondervan, 1995).

8. For initial perspectives, see the entire issue of *Forum* 3, no. 1 (2000). Subsequent installments, though delayed by two years in publication, show that the project is slowly moving forward.

9. The language comes from several of the chapter titles in Ben Witherington III, *The Jesus Quest: The Third Search for the Jew of Nazareth* (Downers Grove, Ill.: InterVarsity Press, 1995).

10. Ben Witherington III, *The Paul Quest: The Renewed Search for the Jew of Tarsus* (Downers Grove, Ill.: InterVarsity Press, 1998).

11. The most ambitious of these endeavors and one of the fairest treatments is Meier, *A Marginal Jew,* with three volumes having appeared by 2002 and at least one more promised.

12. See esp. Stanley E. Porter, *The Criteria for Authenticity in Historical-Jesus Research* (Sheffield, England: Sheffield Academic Press, 2000).

13. N. T. Wright, *Jesus and the Victory of God* (Minneapolis: Fortress, 1996), 131–33; Gerd Theissen and Annette Merz, *The Historical Jesus: A Comprehensive Guide* (Minneapolis: Fortress, 1998), 116–18; Gerd Theissen and Dagmar Winter, *The Quest for the Plausible Jesus: The Question of Criteria* (Louisville: Westminster John Knox Press, 2002).

14. Curiously, this is precisely what some very conservative writers wish we would do. See esp. Robert L. Thomas and F. David Farnell, *The Jesus Crisis: The Inroads of Historical Criticism into Evangelical Scholarship* (Grand Rapids: Kregel, 1998).

15. F. F. Bruce, *The New Testament Documents: Are They Reliable?* (Downers Grove, Ill.: InterVarsity Press, 1960), 16.

16. The standard scholarly introduction to New Testament textual criticism, from which these and many other data may be gleaned, is Kurt

Aland and Barbara Aland, *The Text of the New Testament,* 2d ed. (Grand Rapids: Eerdmans, 1989). For a far briefer survey, requiring no technical knowledge of the field, see David A. Black, *New Testament Textual Criticism: A Concise Guide* (Grand Rapids: Baker, 1994).

17. For Mormonism, see Craig L. Blomberg and Stephen E. Robinson, *How Wide the Divide? A Mormon and an Evangelical in Conversation* (Downers Grove, Ill.: InterVarsity Press, 1997), 55–74. For Islam, see Ghiyathuddin Adelphi and Ernest Hahn, *The Integrity of the Bible according to the Qur'an and the Hadith* (Hyderabad, India: Henry Martyn Institute of Islamic Studies, 1977).

18. Martin Hengel (*The Four Gospels and the One Gospel of Jesus Christ* [Harrisburg, Pa.: Trinity Press International, 2000], esp. 48–56, 96–105) challenges these assumptions, however, and thinks that Mark invented the title and the other Gospel writers consciously followed his model. Hengel's case is suggestive and worth serious consideration, even if ultimately speculative and not provable.

19. For a full discussion of the "external evidence" (the testimony of early Christian writers) concerning the origins of the Gospels and Acts, see the chapters on the four Gospels and Acts in any detailed New Testament introduction, e.g., Donald Guthrie, *New Testament Introduction,* 4th ed. (Downers Grove, Ill.: InterVarsity Press, 1990); or Raymond E. Brown, *An Introduction to the New Testament* (New York: Doubleday, 1997).

20. The standard collection of New Testament apocrypha in English translation is *New Testament Apocrypha,* ed. Wilhelm Schneemelcher, 2d ed., 2 vols. (Louisville: Westminster John Knox Press, 1991–92).

21. For a much fuller discussion, see Craig L. Blomberg, *The Historical Reliability of John's Gospel: Issues and Commentary* (Downers Grove, Ill.: InterVarsity Press, 2001), 22–40.

22. Again, see any of the standard New Testament introductions.

23. For a detailed, persuasive chronology and the relevant references in other ancient sources, see Ben Witherington III, *The Acts of the Apostles: A Socio-Rhetorical Commentary* (Grand Rapids: Eerdmans, 1998), 77–86.

24. Often designated as Q—from the German word *Quelle* for "source." Numerous additional hypotheses about Q by liberal scholars often far outrun what the actual evidence can demonstrate, but the simple hypothesis of the *existence* of such a document in the first century remains probable. See, e.g., Darrell L. Bock, "Questions about Q," in *Rethinking the Synoptic Problem,* ed. David A. Black and David R. Beck (Grand Rapids: Baker, 2001), 41–64.

25. Funk, Hoover, and the Jesus Seminar, *The Five Gospels,* 12–13, 16.

26. See further Robin L. Fox, *The Search for Alexander* (Boston: Little, 1980).

27. A. N. Sherwin-White, *Roman Society and Roman Law in the New Testament* (Oxford: Oxford University Press, 1953), 187.

28. For a good survey of previous approaches and for nuanced conclusions, see Robert Guelich, "The Gospel Genre," in *The Gospel and the Gospels*, ed. Peter Stuhlmacher (Grand Rapids: Eerdmans, 1991), 173–208.

29. See esp. Richard A. Burridge, *What Are the Gospels?* (Cambridge: Cambridge University Press, 1992); Colin Hemer, *The Book of Acts in the Setting of Hellenistic History*, ed. Conrad H. Gempf (Tübingen: Mohr, 1989).

30. Loveday Alexander, *The Preface to Luke's Gospel* (Cambridge: Cambridge University Press, 1993), 21.

31. It is often argued that John's Gospel is considerably less trustworthy historically than the Synoptics but still theologically reliable. One merit of Maurice Casey's *Is John's Gospel True?* (London: Routledge, 1996) is that he recognizes the closer connection between the two, though unfortunately he finds this Gospel unreliable on both counts. For a book-length response, see my *Historical Reliability of John's Gospel.*

32. See esp. Richard Bauckham, ed., *The Gospels for All Christians: Rethinking the Gospel Audiences* (Grand Rapids: Eerdmans, 1998). I am not as convinced as the contributors to this volume that John could presuppose knowledge of the *written* texts of Matthew, Mark, or Luke, but broad awareness of their major contents seems highly probable.

33. See esp. Samuel Byrskog, *Story as History—History as Story* (Tübingen: Mohr, 2000), 235–38; and Derek Tovey, *Narrative Art and Act in the Fourth Gospel* (Sheffield, England: Sheffield Academic Press, 1997), 273.

34. See Darrell L. Bock, "The Words of Jesus in the Gospels: Live, Jive, or Memorex?" in Wilkins and Moreland, *Jesus Under Fire*, 73–99.

35. See further Conrad Gempf, "Public Speaking and Published Accounts," in *The Book of Acts in Its Ancient Literary Setting*, ed. Bruce W. Winter and Andrew D. Clarke (Grand Rapids: Eerdmans, 1993), 259–303.

36. See further David Hill, *New Testament Prophecy* (Atlanta: John Knox, 1979); Christopher Forbes, *Prophecy and Inspired Speech in Early Christianity and Its Hellenistic Environment* (Peabody, Mass.: Hendrickson, 1997).

37. For texts and discussion, see Richard Bauckham, "The Delay of the Parousia," *TynB* 31 (1980): 3–36.

38. See Graham N. Stanton, *Jesus of Nazareth in New Testament Preaching* (Cambridge: Cambridge University Press, 1974), 189.

39. See further, Hemer, *Book of Acts*, 63–100.

40. Bart D. Ehrman, *Jesus: Apocalyptic Prophet of the New Millennium* (Oxford: Oxford University Press, 1999), 51–52.

41. See esp. Birger Gerhardsson, *Memory and Manuscript* (Lund, Sweden: Gleerup, 1961), 43–66. Also important are two German works never translated into English: Rainer Riesner, *Jesus als Lehrer* (Tübingen: Mohr, 1981); and A. F. Zimmermann, *Die urchristlichen Lehrer* (Tübingen: Mohr, 1984).

42. See esp. A. B. Lord, "The Gospels as Oral Traditional Literature," in *The Relationships among the Gospels*, ed. William O. Walker, Jr. (San Antonio: Trinity University Press, 1978), 33–91; and Kenneth E. Bailey, "Informal Controlled Oral Tradition and the Synoptic Gospels," *AJT* 5 (1991): 34–53. James D. G. Dunn's new work (*Jesus Remembered* [Grand Rapids: Eerdmans, 2003], 173–254) makes more use of these findings than any other historical Jesus book has.

43. See esp. Alan Millard, *Reading and Writing in the Time of Jesus* (Sheffield, England: Sheffield Academic Press, 2000), 210–29.

44. Indeed, the seeds for this organization stem from Jesus' ministry itself. See esp. Meier, *Marginal Jew*, 3:148–63.

45. E.g., C. Dennis McKinsey, *The Encyclopedia of Biblical Errancy* (Amherst, N.Y.: Prometheus, 1995).

46. Craig L. Blomberg, *The Historical Reliability of the Gospels* (Downers Grove, Ill.: InterVarsity Press, 1987), 113–89; idem, *Historical Reliability of John's Gospel*.

47. Most of the wording of this paragraph is borrowed from excerpts of Craig L. Blomberg, "Where Do We Start Studying Jesus?" in Wilkins and Moreland, *Jesus Under Fire*, 35.

48. Paul Merkley, "The Gospels as Historical Testimony," *EvQ* 58 (1986): 328–36.

49. Stanley E. Porter, " 'In the Vicinity of Jericho': Luke 18:35 in the Light of Its Synoptic Parallels," *BBR* 2 (1992): 91–104.

50. See further Craig L. Blomberg, "The Legitimacy and Limits of Harmonization," in *Hermeneutics, Authority, and Canon*, ed. D. A. Carson and John D. Woodbridge (Grand Rapids: Zondervan, 1986; reprint, Grand Rapids: Baker, 1991), 135–74.

51. Blomberg, *Historical Reliability of John's Gospel*.

52. For these and other examples, and for all of the scriptural references attached to each of these items, see my *Historical Reliability of the Gospels*, 156–59.

53. For a good discussion of these and related circumstances, see Ben

Witherington III, *John's Wisdom: A Commentary on the Fourth Gospel* (Louisville: Westminster John Knox Press, 1995), 27–41.

54. For these and numerous other examples of both forms of interlocking, see Leon Morris, *Studies in the Fourth Gospel* (Grand Rapids: Eerdmans, 1969), 40–63; and Richard Bauckham, "John for Readers of Mark," in Bauckham, *The Gospels for All Christians*, 147–71.

55. German original 1950. Translated into English as Phillip Vielhauer, "On the 'Paulinism' of Acts," in *Studies in Luke-Acts*, ed. Leander E. Keck and J. Louis Martyn (Nashville: Abingdon, 1966), 33–50.

56. David Wenham, "Acts and the Pauline Corpus II: The Evidence of Parallels," in Winter and Clarke, *Acts in Its Ancient Literary Setting*, 215–58. See also Stanley E. Porter, *The Paul of Acts* (Tübingen: Mohr, 1999). For a response to an array of much more minor supposed contradictions of detail between Acts and the epistles, see Hemer, *Book of Acts*, 244–307.

57. See, e.g., Darrell L. Bock, *Luke* (Grand Rapids: Baker, 1996), 2:1284–85.

58. For an excellent study of numerous "pre-formed traditions" in all portions of the New Testament that the writers of Scripture may have taken over largely unaltered, see E. Earle Ellis, *The Making of the New Testament Documents* (Leiden: Brill, 1999). Ellis probably overestimates how many of these can be identified with confidence, but even if a substantial minority of those he discusses prove genuine, his conclusions concerning the conservative nature of New Testament tradition follow logically.

59. See Eugene E. Lemcio, *The Past of Jesus in the Gospels* (Cambridge: Cambridge University Press, 1991).

60. See, e.g., Anthony C. Thiselton, *The First Epistle to the Corinthians* (Grand Rapids: Eerdmans, 2000), 525–26.

61. The fullest compilation of all this data is now conveniently accessible in Robert E. Van Voorst, *Jesus Outside the New Testament: An Introduction to the Ancient Evidence* (Grand Rapids: Eerdmans, 2000).

62. Translations are taken from the standard critical edition found in the Loeb Classical Library.

63. See esp. Meier, *A Marginal Jew*, 1:56–88.

64. On which, see esp. Graham N. Stanton, "Jesus of Nazareth: A Magician and a False Prophet Who Deceived God's People?" in *Jesus of Nazareth: Lord and Christ*, ed. Joel B. Green and Max Turner (Grand Rapids: Eerdmans, 1994), 164–80.

65. Much of the language in this section on rabbinic traditions comes from my *Historical Reliability of the Gospels*, 198–99. For more detail, see Graham H. Twelftree, "Jesus in Jewish Traditions," in vol. 5 of *Gospel Per-*

spectives, ed. David Wenham (Sheffield, England: JSOT, 1985), 289–341, from which the translations used above are also adopted.

66. Murray J. Harris, "References to Jesus in Early Classical Authors," in Wenham, *Gospel Perspectives*, 5:356. The overall article (pp. 343–68) provides more detailed discussion of these references along with the translations adopted here.

67. Van Voorst, *Jesus Outside the New Testament*, 66.

68. For recent examples of such claims, see the survey in ibid., 1–17.

69. For a good overview, see Paul W. Barnett, *Jesus and the Logic of History* (Grand Rapids: Eerdmans, 1997; reprint, Downers Grove, Ill.: Inter-Varsity Press, 2001), 59–89.

70. Excerpting and abbreviating from Hemer, *Book of Acts*, 101–58.

71. See also, classically, James Smith, *The Voyage and Shipwreck of Saint Paul*, 4th ed. (Minneapolis: James Family Christian Publishers, 1880).

72. For a standard evangelical presentation, see F. F. Bruce, *Paul: Apostle of the Heart Set Free* (Grand Rapids: Eerdmans, 1977), 475.

73. Not surprisingly, this is the one speech in Acts that most resembles the Paul of the epistles. It is also the only place where the audiences are similar—an already established Christian church—so this is exactly what we should expect.

74. Jews did produce a small number of fictitious novels about allegedly contemporary individuals, but all of them contain various historical anachronisms that betray their true nature and origin. The fullest collection appears in *Ancient Jewish Novels: An Anthology*, ed. and trans. Lawrence M. Wills (Oxford: Oxford University Press, 2002).

75. For key, recent book-length treatments on the Gospels, see R. Arav and J. Rousseau, *Jesus and His World: An Archaeological and Cultural Dictionary* (Minneapolis: Fortress, 1995); Bargil Pixner, *With Jesus through Galilee according to the Fifth Gospel* (Collegeville, Minn.: Liturgical, 1996) (the "Fifth Gospel" is the witness of archaeology); and J. L. Reed, *Archaeology and the Galilean Jesus* (Harrisburg, Pa.: Trinity Press International, 2000). For the archaeology of the New Testament more generally, with sizable sections on the Gospels and Acts, see John McRay, *Archaeology and the New Testament* (Grand Rapids: Baker, 1991); Jack Finegan, *The Archeology of the New Testament*, rev. ed. (Princeton: Princeton University Press, 1992); and W. H. C. Frend, *The Archaeology of Early Christianity: A History* (Minneapolis: Fortress, 1996).

76. A strong case can be made, however, for locating Herod's palace on the west side of Old Jerusalem near the present-day Jaffa Gate. This would then locate the Via Dolorosa and Christ's "stations of the cross" in

almost the opposite direction from where they have traditionally been identified.

77. For a dissenting view, see William Horbury, "The 'Caiaphas' Ossuaries and Joseph Caiaphas," *PEQ* 126 (1994): 32–48.

78. See esp. Hershel Shanks and Ben Witherington III, *The Brother of Jesus* (San Francisco: HarperSanFrancisco, 2003).

79. So especially Richard A. Batey, *Jesus and the Forgotten City* (Grand Rapids: Baker, 1991).

80. See further Stanton, *Gospel Truth?* 119–20.

81. Various portions of this section on the archaeology of the Gospels reuse, reorganize, and abbreviate language found in Craig L. Blomberg, *Jesus and the Gospels: An Introduction and Survey* (Nashville: Broadman and Holman, 1997), 367–70.

82. On which, see, classically, Sir William Ramsay, *St. Paul the Traveler and Roman Citizen,* ed. and rev. Mark Wilson, 15th ed. (London: Hodder & Stoughton, 1925; rev. ed., Grand Rapids: Kregel, 2001).

83. In fact, because "Areopagus" can mean the city council as well as the actual Mars Hill site, many scholars think Paul spoke to these officials somewhere near the Stoa, where visiting philosophers regularly conversed.

84. The classic study is again that of Sir William Ramsay, *The Letters to the Seven Churches of Asia and Their Place in the Plan of the Apocalypse* (London: Hodder & Stoughton, 1904). An even more valuable modern study is Colin J. Hemer, *The Letters to the Seven Churches of Asia in Their Local Setting* (Sheffield, England: JSOT, 1986).

85. M. J. S. Rudwick and E. M. B. Green, "The Laodicean Lukewarmness," *ExpT* 69 (1957–58): 176–78.

86. For more on this thorny problem, see Craig L. Blomberg, "Quirinius," in *International Standard Bible Encyclopedia,* rev. and ed. Edgar W. Smith, Jr. (Grand Rapids: Eerdmans, 1986), 4:12–13.

87. But the two Theudases may not be the same. See esp. Witherington, *Acts,* 235–39.

88. For the view that Papias's apparent disparagement of written texts applied only to nonapostolic sources, see A. F. Walls, "Papias and Oral Tradition," *VC* 21 (1967): 137–40.

89. The best modern English translation and introduction is *The Apostolic Fathers,* ed. and rev. Michael W. Holmes (Grand Rapids: Baker, 1992).

90. See further Blomberg, *Historical Reliability of the Gospels,* 202–8, and the literature cited there.

91. G. K. Beale, "The Use of Daniel in the Synoptic Eschatological Dis-

course and in the Book of Revelation," in Wenham, *Gospel Perspectives*, 5:129–53.

92. Louis A. Vos, *The Synoptic Traditions in the Apocalypse* (Kampen: Kok, 1965).

93. For considerably longer lists, see Robert H. Gundry, " 'Verba Christi' in 1 Peter: Their Implications Concerning the Authorship of 1 Peter and the Authenticity of the Gospel Tradition," *NTS* 13 (1966–67): 336–50; and idem, "Further Verba on Verba Christi in First Peter," *Bib* 55 (1974): 211–32.

94. Helpfully tabulated in chart form in Peter H. Davids, *The Epistle of James* (Grand Rapids: Eerdmans, 1982), 47–48.

95. So especially David Wenham, "Paul's Use of the Jesus Tradition: Three Samples," in idem, *Gospel Perspectives*, 5:7–15.

96. See, e.g., Raymond F. Collins, *First Corinthians* (Collegeville, Minn.: Liturgical, 1999), 425–26.

97. For references, see Blomberg, *Historical Reliability of the Gospels*, 222. Scattered bits of the wording of this subsection on Paul are taken from pp. 223–28, which also offers a fuller treatment of the topic.

98. For more on identifying such creeds, see Ralph P. Martin, *New Testament Foundations* (Grand Rapids: Eerdmans, 1978), 2:249–75.

99. For detailed elaboration, see Larry W. Hurtado, *Lord Jesus Christ: Devotion to Jesus in Earliest Christianity* (Grand Rapids: Eerdmans, 2003).

100. Gerd Lüdemann with Alf Özen, *What Really Happened to Jesus: A Historical Approach to the Resurrection* (Louisville: Westminster John Knox Press, 1995), 15.

101. The best recent philosophical discussion of miracles is Douglas Geivett and Gary R. Habermas, eds., *In Defense of Miracles: A Comprehensive Case for God's Action in History* (Downers Grove, Ill.: InterVarsity Press, 1997). The best recent exegetical study of Jesus' miracles is Graham H. Twelftree, *Jesus the Miracle Worker: A Historical and Theological Study* (Downers Grove, Ill.: InterVarsity Press, 1999).

102. Rudolf Bultmann, "New Testament and Mythology," in *Kerygma and Myth*, ed. H.-W. Bartsch (London: SPCK, 1953), 4.

103. For a more detailed exposition of Hume, see Colin Brown, *Miracles and the Critical Mind* (Grand Rapids: Eerdmans, 1984), 79–100.

104. A succinct summary appears in Roy A. Harrisville and Walter Sundberg, *The Bible in Modern Culture: Theology and Historical-Critical Method from Spinoza to Käsemann* (Grand Rapids: Eerdmans, 1995), 89–110.

105. See already Peter Medawar, *The Limits of Science* (San Francisco: Harper & Row, 1984).

106. See esp. Meier, *A Marginal Jew*, 2:520–21.

107. One of the best philosophical defenses in modern times of miracle is Richard Swinburne, *The Concept of Miracle* (New York: St. Martin's, 1970).

108. See, e.g., W. K. C. Guthrie, *The Greeks and Their Gods* (Boston: Beacon, 1950), 247–53. Lucian's ancient satires themselves often disclose the role of "human manufacture" in alleged Greco-Roman miracles. For an excellent study of the supposed parallels to the Gospel miracles, see Meier, *A Marginal Jew*, 2:576–601.

109. See further Harold Remus, *Pagan-Christian Conflict over Miracle in the Second Century* (Cambridge, Mass.: Philadelphia Patristic Foundation, 1983).

110. Meier, *A Marginal Jew*, 2:630.

111. On the question of historicity, see Pinchas Lapide, *The Resurrection of Jesus: A Jewish Perspective* (Minneapolis: Augsburg, 1983); John Wenham, *Easter Enigma: Are the Resurrection Accounts in Conflict?* (Grand Rapids: Zondervan, 1984); and William L. Craig, *Assessing the New Testament Evidence for the Historicity of the Resurrection of Jesus* (Lewiston, N.Y.: Mellen, 1989).

112. N. T. Wright, *The Resurrection of the Son of God* (Minneapolis: Fortress, 2003).

113. See esp. Murray J. Harris, *From Grave to Glory: Resurrection in the New Testament* (Grand Rapids: Zondervan, 1990). For a response to exceptions to the current trends, see Gary R. Habermas, "The Late Twentieth-Century Resurgence of Naturalistic Responses to Jesus' Resurrection," *TrinJ* 22 (2001): 179–96.

114. For elaboration, see the segments authored by William Lane Craig in two books containing published versions of his debates (with Gerd Lüdemann and John Dominic Crossan, respectively): Paul Copan and Ronald K. Tacelli, eds., *Jesus' Resurrection: Fact or Figment?* (Downers Grove, Ill.: InterVarsity Press, 2000); and Paul Copan, ed., *Will the Real Jesus Please Stand Up?* (Grand Rapids: Baker, 1998).

CHAPTER 2:
WAS PAUL THE TRUE FOUNDER OF CHRISTIANITY?

1. For both developments, see the historical survey in Victor P. Furnish, "The Jesus-Paul Debate: From Baur to Bultmann," in *Paul and Jesus: Collected Essays*, ed. A. J. M. Wedderburn (Sheffield, England: JSOT, 1989), 17–50.

2. For these quotations and for excerpts of both men's writings on

Paul, see *The Writings of St. Paul: A Norton Critical Edition,* ed. Wayne A. Meeks (New York: Norton, 1972), 288–302.

3. See esp. Rudolf Bultmann, "Jesus and Paul," in *Existence and Faith,* ed. and trans. Schubert M. Ogden (New York: Meridian, 1960), 183–201.

4. In addition to the standard commentaries, see esp. the otherwise fairly liberal study of C. Wolff, "The Apostolic Knowledge of Christ: Exegetical Reflections on 2 Corinthians 5.14ff.," in Wedderburn, *Paul and Jesus,* 81–98.

5. F. F. Bruce, *Paul and Jesus* (Grand Rapids: Baker, 1974); J. W. Fraser, *Jesus and Paul: Paul as Interpreter of Jesus from Harnack to Kümmel* (Appleford, England: Marcham Manor Press, 1974).

6. See, e.g., Victor P. Furnish, *Jesus according to Paul* (Cambridge: Cambridge University Press, 1993).

7. David Wenham, *Paul: Follower of Jesus or Founder of Christianity?* (Grand Rapids: Eerdmans, 1995); idem, *Paul and Jesus: The True Story* (Grand Rapids: Eerdmans, 2002). See also idem, "Paul's Use of the Jesus Tradition: Three Samples," in vol. 5 of *Gospel Perspectives,* ed. David Wenham (Sheffield, England: JSOT, 1985), 7–37; idem, "The Story of Jesus Known to Paul," in *Jesus of Nazareth: Lord and Christ,* ed. Joel B. Green and Max Turner (Grand Rapids: Eerdmans, 1994), 297–311; and idem, "From Jesus to Paul—via Luke," in *The Gospel to the Nations: Perspectives on Paul's Mission,* ed. Peter Bolt and Mark Thompson (Downers Grove, Ill.: InterVarsity Press, 2000), 83–97.

8. Michael D. Goulder, *Paul and the Competing Mission in Corinth* (Peabody, Mass.: Hendrickson, 2001).

9. Gerd Lüdemann, *Paul: The Founder of Christianity* (Amherst, N.Y.: Prometheus, 2002).

10. The title of a book by Maurice Casey on the development of New Testament christology (Louisville: Westminster John Knox Press, 1991).

11. See, e.g., I. Howard Marshall, *Last Supper and Lord's Supper* (Grand Rapids: Eerdmans, 1980), 30–56, and the survey of research contained there.

12. See further Anthony C. Thiselton, *The First Epistle to the Corinthians* (Grand Rapids: Eerdmans, 2000), esp. 692–98. Thiselton notes that patristic authors understood the text in this fashion as well (692).

13. For similar commentary on all these verses in 1 Corinthians 7, see esp. Gordon D. Fee, *The First Epistle to the Corinthians* (Grand Rapids: Eerdmans, 1987), esp. 291.

14. *Contra* the otherwise excellent study of David L. Dungan (*The Sayings of Jesus in the Churches of Paul* [Philadelphia: Fortress, 1971]) on the sayings of Jesus in both 1 Corinthians 7 and 9.

15. On which, see esp. Michael Thompson, *Clothed with Christ: The Example and Teaching of Jesus in Romans 12.1–15.13* (Sheffield, England: JSOT, 1991).

16. On each of these allusions, see also Wenham, *Paul*, 251–53.

17. Robert W. Funk, Roy W. Hoover, and the Jesus Seminar, *The Five Gospels: The Search for the Authentic Words of Jesus* (New York: Macmillan, 1993), 102.

18. Bruce (*Paul and Jesus*, 71) also points out the probable symbolism of the sending of the seventy in Luke 10 in foreshadowing the Gentile mission, of which Paul became the prime mover in the early church.

19. For further possible allusions to the missionary discourses of Matthew 10 and Luke 10, see Wenham, *Paul*, 190–99.

20. See further ibid., 320–21.

21. The parallels are even closer once one recognizes that the "rapture" in 1 Thess. 4:17 is most likely post-tribulational—that is, at the same time as the public return of Christ. See, e.g., Bob Gundry, *First the Antichrist* (Grand Rapids: Baker, 1997).

22. On which, see esp. David Wenham (*The Rediscovery of Jesus' Eschatological Discourse* [Sheffield, England: JSOT, 1984]), who demonstrates the plausibility of one connected sermon behind most of Matthew's, Mark's, and Luke's various apocalyptic sayings of Jesus.

23. See further David Wenham, "Paul and the Synoptic Apocalypse," in vol. 2 of *Gospel Perspectives*, ed. R. T. France and David Wenham (Sheffield, England: JSOT, 1981), 345–75.

24. Among recent scholars, Seyoon Kim ("Jesus, Sayings of," in *Dictionary of Paul and His Letters*, ed. Gerald F. Hawthorne, Ralph P. Martin, and Daniel G. Reid [Downers Grove, Ill.: InterVarsity Press, 1993]), with his chart of "Possible Echoes of Sayings of Jesus" (p. 481), seems a bit overconfident in his list of thirty-one items.

25. For surveys of similar lists from quite different perspectives, compare Dale C. Allison, Jr., "The Pauline Epistles and the Synoptic Gospels: The Pattern of the Parallels," *NTS* 28 (1982): 1–32; and Frans Neirynck, "Paul and the Sayings of Jesus," in *L'Apôtre Paul: Personnalité, style et conception du ministère*, ed. Albert Vanhoye (Louvain: Louvain University Press, 1986), 265–321.

26. See the chart in Peter Richardson, "The Thunderbolt in Q and the Wise Man in Corinth," in *From Jesus to Paul*, ed. Peter Richardson and John C. Hurd (Waterloo, Ont.: Wilfrid Laurier Press, 1984), 96. For a longer but more speculative treatment of possible allusions to Jesus' teachings in 1 Corinthians 1–4, see Biorn Fjärstedt, *Synoptic Tradition in 1 Corinthians* (Uppsala, Sweden: Teologiska Institutionen, 1974).

27. For still more possible allusions in Paul to this discourse, see Wenham, *Paul,* 199.

28. See, e.g., Ben F. Meyer, *The Aims of Jesus* (London: SCM, 1979), 185–97.

29. Thus Maurice A. Robinson, "ΣΠΕΡΜΟΛΟΓΟΣ: Did Paul Preach from Jesus' Parables?" *Bib* 56 (1975): 231–40.

30. See esp. Larry W. Hurtado, "Jesus as Lordly Example in Philippians 2:5–11," in Richardson and Hurd, *From Jesus to Paul,* 113–26.

31. So especially Christopher Marshall, "Paul and Jesus: Continuity or Discontinuity?" *Stimulus* 5, no. 4 (1997): 32–42.

32. Donald H. Akenson, *Saint Saul: A Skeleton Key to the Historical Jesus* (Oxford: Oxford University Press, 2000), 224.

33. Stanley E. Porter, "Images of Christ in Paul's Letters," in *Images of Christ: Ancient and Modern,* ed. Stanley E. Porter, Michael A. Hayes, and David Tombs (Sheffield, England: Sheffield Academic Press, 1997), 98–99. See also J. P. Arnold, "The Relationship of Paul to Jesus," in *Hillel and Jesus: Comparative Studies of Two Major Religious Leaders,* ed. James H. Charlesworth and Loren L. Johns (Minneapolis: Fortress, 1997), 256–88.

34. Most commentators correctly argue that all that can be demonstrated certainly from this reference is Paul's belief in Jesus' full humanity. But Timothy George (*Galatians* [Nashville: Broadman & Holman, 1994], 302–3), whose commentary deals more with broader systematic and historical-theological concerns than most, rightly observes that "it is inconceivable that Paul, the travel companion of Luke, would not have known about the virginal conception of Jesus. The fact that he nowhere mentions the virgin birth in his letters could only mean that it was so universally accepted among the Christian churches to which he wrote that he deemed no elaboration or defense of it necessary. As J. G. Machen noted, 'The virgin birth does seem to be implied in the profoundest way in the entire view which Paul holds of the Lord Jesus Christ.'"

35. Wenham, *Paul and Jesus,* 66–67.

36. Alfred Plummer, *A Critical and Exegetical Commentary on the First Epistle of St Paul to the Corinthians* (Edinburgh: T & T Clark, 1911), 22.

37. See esp. John P. Meier, *A Marginal Jew: Rethinking the Historical Jesus* (New York: Doubleday, 1991), 1:278–85, 309–15.

38. See esp. Gillian Clark, "The Social Status of Paul," *ExpT* 96 (1985): 110–11.

39. See esp. A. D. A. Moses, *Matthew's Transfiguration Story and Jewish-Christian Controversy* (Sheffield, England: Sheffield Academic Press, 1996).

40. David Wenham and A. D. A. Moses, "'There Are Some Standing Here . . .': Did They Become the 'Reputed Pillars' of the Jerusalem Church? Some Reflections on Mark 9:1, Galatians 2:9, and the Transfiguration," *NovT* 36 (1994): 146–63.

41. See further Christian Wolff, "Humility and Self-Denial in Jesus' Life and Message and in the Apostolic Existence of Paul," in Wedderburn, *Paul and Jesus*, 145–60.

42. David Stanley, "Imitation in Paul's Letters: Its Significance for His Relationship to Jesus and to His Own Christian Foundations," in Richardson and Hurd, *From Jesus to Paul*, 127–41.

43. Akenson, *Saint Saul*, 173.

44. James D. G. Dunn, "Paul's Knowledge of the Jesus Tradition," in *Christus Bezeugen*, ed. Karl Kertelge, Traugott Holtz, and Claus-Peter März (Leipzig: St. Benno, 1989), 194.

45. Several of these points are laid out more clearly and systematically in Rainer Riesner ("Paulus und die Jesus-Überlieferung," in *Evangelium, Schriftauslegung, Kirche*, ed. Jostein Ådna, Scott J. Hafemann, and Otfried Hofius [Göttingen: Vandenhoeck und Ruprecht, 1997], 356–65) than in any English-language source of which I am aware.

46. C. H. Dodd, *The Apostolic Preaching and Its Developments* (London: Hodder & Stoughton, 1936), 54–56.

47. Charles F. D. Moule, "Jesus in New Testament Kerygma," in *Verborum Veritas*, ed. Otto Bücher and Klaus Haacker (Wuppertal, Germany: Brockhaus, 1970), 15–26.

48. See further Donald A. Hagner, "The Sayings of Jesus in the Apostolic Fathers and Justin Martyr," in Wenham, *Gospel Perspectives*, 5:233–68.

49. A key theme stressed throughout Herman Ridderbos, *Paul and Jesus* (Grand Rapids: Baker, 1958). See also Eduard Schweizer, "The Testimony to Jesus in the Early Christian Community," *HBT* 7 (1985): 77–98.

50. See, e.g., Paul W. Barnett, "The Importance of Paul for the Historical Jesus," *Crux* 29 (1993): 29–32. For a survey of current trends in interpreting Paul more broadly, see esp. Ben Witherington III, *The Paul Quest: The Renewed Search for the Jew of Tarsus* (Downers Grove, Ill.: InterVarsity Press, 1998).

51. Dunn, "Paul's Knowledge," 206–7.

52. Traugott Holtz, "Paul and the Oral Gospel Tradition," in *Jesus and the Oral Gospel Tradition*, ed. Henry Wansbrough (Sheffield, England: JSOT, 1991), 380–93.

53. It is interesting to compare the two most recent evangelical theologies of Paul. James D. G. Dunn (*The Theology of Paul the Apostle* [Grand

Rapids: Eerdmans, 1998]) works largely with the undisputed letters precisely because the others are disputed, while Thomas R. Schreiner (*Paul: Apostle of God's Glory in Christ* [Downers Grove, Ill.: InterVarsity Press, 2001]) equally deliberately includes all thirteen letters attributed to Paul in the New Testament. Nevertheless, the pictures that emerge from the two studies are in most cases quite consistent with each other. And what differences do appear stem largely from considerations other than whether to include the six disputed letters or not.

54. See James D. G. Dunn and Alan M. Suggate, *The Justice of God* (Carlisle, England: Paternoster, 1993); Elsa Tamez, *The Amnesty of Grace: Justification by Faith from a Latin American Perspective* (Nashville: Abingdon, 1993). Spanish speakers can often appreciate this point better than English speakers, since *justicia* regularly translates *dikaiosunē* in Spanish-language translations. As in Greek, the one word is used for both concepts.

55. See esp. Ben Witherington III, *The Christology of Jesus* (Philadelphia: Fortress, 1990), 191–215.

56. George Johnston, " 'Kingdom of God' Sayings in Paul's Letters," in Richardson and Hurd, *From Jesus to Paul*, 143–56.

57. On which, see esp. Craig L. Blomberg, " 'Your Faith Has Made You Whole': The Evangelical Liberation Theology of Jesus," in Green and Turner, *Jesus of Nazareth*, 75–93.

58. F. F. Bruce, "Justification by Faith in the Non-Pauline Writings of the New Testament," *EvQ* 24 (1952): 66–69.

59. See esp. George E. Ladd, *A Theology of the New Testament*, rev. Donald A. Hagner (Grand Rapids: Eerdmans, 1993), 290–95.

60. No scholar has pursued this campaign of charges more consistently than the Finnish scholar Heikki Räisänen. See esp. his *Jesus, Paul, and Torah: Collected Essays* (Sheffield, England: JSOT, 1992).

61. See esp. Douglas J. Moo, "Jesus and the Authority of the Mosaic Law," *JSNT* 20 (1984): 3–49.

62. J. Louis Martyn, *Galatians* (New York: Doubleday, 1997), 549.

63. See esp. throughout Peter Stuhlmacher, *Biblische Theologie des Neuen Testaments*, 2 vols. (Göttingen: Vandenhoeck und Ruprecht, 1992–99), unfortunately not yet translated into English.

64. The best study of the full range of issues associated with Sabbath/Sunday observance biblically, theologically, and historically is D. A. Carson, ed., *From Sabbath to Lord's Day* (Grand Rapids: Zondervan, 1982).

65. See esp. Dale C. Allison, Jr., *Jesus of Nazareth: Millenarian Prophet* (Minneapolis: Fortress, 1998), 172–216; Vincent L. Wimbush, *Paul: The Worldly Ascetic* (Macon, Ga.: Mercer University Press, 1987).

66. Though found in John, this verse is often seen as the one core part of the passage that is authentic. Not a few scholars believe that John 2:12–25 is *more* authentic than the comparable Synoptic accounts of the temple cleansing. See further Craig L. Blomberg, *The Historical Reliability of John's Gospel: Issues and Commentary* (Downers Grove, Ill.: InterVarsity Press, 2001), 87–91.

67. Though again commentators differ, some thinking a hedonistic Gentile practice is in view here.

68. Cited in Ladd, *Theology,* 104.

69. See above, pp. 79, 161 n. 28. See also Gerhard Maier, "The Church in the Gospel of Matthew: Hermeneutical Analysis of the Current Debate," in *Biblical Interpretation and the Church: The Problem of Contextualization,* ed. D. A. Carson (Nashville: Nelson, 1985), 45–63.

70. See esp. throughout vol. 3 of Meier, *A Marginal Jew,* summarized on pp. 626–32. More generally, see Richard Bauckham, "Kingdom and Church according to Jesus and Paul," *HBT* 18 (1996): 1–26.

71. See Craig L. Blomberg, *Neither Poverty nor Riches: A Biblical Theology of Possessions* (Leicester, England: InterVarsity Press, 1999), 111–46. For comparable material in Paul, see pp. 177–212.

72. Even the most skeptical portraits of Jesus regularly acknowledge this central element to his ministry. See, e.g., throughout J. Dominic Crossan, *The Historical Jesus: The Life of a Mediterranean Jewish Peasant* (San Francisco: HarperSanFrancisco, 1991).

73. Namely, that a critical minimum of authentic Jesus material can be determined by accepting sayings of Jesus in the Gospels that neither the Judaism that preceded him nor the Christianity that followed him likely would have invented.

74. For more on Jesus' overtures to non-Jewish people, see C. H. H. Scobie, "Jesus or Paul? The Origin of the Universal Mission of the Christian Church," in Richardson and Hurd, *From Jesus to Paul,* 47–61.

75. Alexander J. M. Wedderburn, "Paul and Jesus: Similarity and Continuity," in idem, *Paul and Jesus,* 139.

76. J. M. G. Barclay, "Jesus and Paul," in *Dictionary of Paul and His Letters,* ed. Gerald F. Hawthorne, Ralph P. Martin, and Daniel G. Reid (Downers Grove, Ill.: InterVarsity Press, 1993), 502.

77. Wenham, *Paul,* 190.

78. See esp. Kathleen Corley, *Women and the Historical Jesus* (Santa Rosa, Calif.: Polebridge, 2002); more briefly, Grant R. Osborne, "Women in Jesus' Ministry," *WTJ* 51 (1989): 259–91.

79. Of course, Pauline authorship of the Pastoral Epistles is heavily

disputed. But the best explanation of Paul's restriction in 1 Cor. 14:34–35 on women speaking also relies on understanding them outside an elder's role in evaluating prophecy. For all of the material in this section on Paul, and for the detailed exegesis to back up my generalizations, see Craig L. Blomberg, "Neither Hierarchicalist nor Egalitarian: Gender Roles in Paul," in *Two Views on Women in Ministry,* ed. James R. Beck and Craig L. Blomberg (Grand Rapids: Zondervan, 2001), 329–72.

80. Perhaps the best study of a number of these categories, including more detail, is Witherington, *Christology of Jesus.* See also throughout N. T. Wright, *Jesus and the Victory of God* (Minneapolis: Fortress, 1996).

81. See esp. Meier, *A Marginal Jew,* 2:100–116.

82. For extensive detail, see ibid., 509–1038.

83. See esp. E. P. Sanders, *Jesus and Judaism* (Philadelphia: Fortress, 1985), 61–76.

84. For this original meaning and one possible network of historical developments, see Bruce D. Chilton, *A Feast of Meanings: Eucharistic Theologies from Jesus through Johannine Circles* (Leiden: Brill, 1994).

85. See in detail Meier, *A Marginal Jew,* 3:289–613.

86. See esp. throughout Meyer, *Aims of Jesus.*

87. See esp. Philip B. Payne, "Jesus' Implicit Claim to Deity in His Parables," *TrinJ,* n.s., 2 (1981): 3–23.

88. For a judicious assessment of competing claims about the significance of Abba, see Scot McKnight, *A New Vision for Israel: The Teachings of Jesus in National Context* (Grand Rapids: Eerdmans, 1999), 49–65.

89. Nevertheless, a suggestive case can be made for linking "Son of Man" with Paul's "new Adam" christology. See esp. Rom. 5:12–21 and 1 Cor. 15:22, 45–49.

90. See esp. Seyoon Kim, *The Son of Man as the Son of God* (Grand Rapids: Eerdmans, 1985).

91. See esp. Richard Bauckham, "The Sonship of the Historical Jesus in Christology," *SJT* 31 (1978): 245–60.

92. Craig L. Blomberg, "Messiah in the New Testament," in *Israel's Messiah in the Bible and the Dead Sea Scrolls,* ed. Richard S. Hess and M. Daniel Carroll R. (Grand Rapids: Baker, 2003), 125–32. In this book, however, simply for the sake of variety, I *have* adopted the post–New Testament practice of using "Jesus" and "Christ" largely interchangeably as two different names for the same man from Nazareth.

93. See esp. Martin Hengel, *Studies in Early Christology* (Edinburgh: T & T Clark, 1995), 119–225.

94. See further Ben Witherington III, *The Many Faces of the Christ: The*

Christologies of the New Testament and Beyond (New York: Crossroad, 1998), esp. 103–26.

95. See, respectively, Hans F. Bayer, *Jesus' Predictions of Vindication and Resurrection* (Tübingen: Mohr, 1986); and Sydney H. T. Page, "The Authenticity of the Ransom Logion (Mark 10:45b)," in vol. 1 of *Gospel Perspectives,* ed. R. T. France and David Wenham (Sheffield, England: JSOT, 1980), 137–61.

96. See, e.g., N. T. Wright, *What St. Paul Really Said* (Grand Rapids: Eerdmans), 135–50, esp. 140–42.

97. For book-length detail on these and related items, see Ben Witherington III, *Jesus, Paul, and the End of the World* (Downers Grove, Ill.: InterVarsity Press, 1992).

98. Seyoon Kim, *The Origin of Paul's Gospel* (Grand Rapids: Eerdmans, 1981). See also Richard N. Longenecker, "A Realized Hope, a New Commitment, and a Developed Proclamation: Paul and Jesus," in *The Road from Damascus,* ed. Richard N. Longenecker (Grand Rapids: Eerdmans, 1997), 18–42.

99. Richard N. Longenecker, *Galatians* (Dallas: Word, 1990), 37–38.

100. See further Wendell Willis, "An Irenic View of Christian Origins: Theological Continuity from Jesus to Paul in W. R. Farmer's Writings," in *Jesus, the Gospels, and the Church,* ed. E. P. Sanders (Macon, Ga.: Mercer University Press, 1987), 265–86.

101. Allison, "The Pauline Epistles," 25.

Chapter 3:
How Is the Christian to Apply the New Testament to Life?

1. At an introductory level, see esp. Gordon D. Fee and Douglas Stuart, *How to Read the Bible for All Its Worth,* rev. ed. (Grand Rapids: Zondervan, 1993). For more detail, see William W. Klein, Craig L. Blomberg, and Robert L. Hubbard, Jr., *Introduction to Biblical Interpretation,* rev. ed. (Nashville: Nelson, forthcoming).

2. Important, recent exceptions include Jack Kuhatschek, *Taking the Guesswork Out of Applying the Bible* (Grand Rapids: Zondervan, 1990); David Veerman, *How to Apply the Bible* (Wheaton, Ill.: Tyndale, 1993); and Daniel M. Doriani, *Putting the Truth to Work: The Theory and Practice of Biblical Application* (Phillipsburg, N.J.: Presbyterian & Reformed, 2001).

3. Klein, Blomberg, and Hubbard, *Introduction to Biblical Interpretation,* chap. 10; Craig L. Blomberg, "The Diversity of Literary Genres in the

New Testament," in *Interpreting the New Testament*, ed. David A. Black and David S. Dockery (Nashville: Broadman & Holman, 2001), 272–95.

4. Klein, Blomberg, and Hubbard, *Introduction to Biblical Interpretation*, chap. 12.

5. Published by Zondervan in Grand Rapids, Michigan.

6. In both instances published by InterVarsity Press in Downers Grove, Illinois, and Leicester, England. Inter-Varsity Press UK originated the Bible Speaks Today; InterVarsity Press US initiated the InterVarsity Press New Testament Commentary Series.

7. At a very basic level, many of the volumes in the Holman New Testament Commentary series (Nashville: Broadman & Holman) prove helpful, as do the expositions of Kent Hughes (Wheaton, Ill.: Crossway) and D. A. Carson (Grand Rapids: Baker), neither of which is part of any formal series. And numerous single volumes on specific NT books, also not attached to series, at times produce good, thorough application—e.g., Eugene H. Peterson, *Reversed Thunder: The Revelation of John and the Praying Imagination* (San Francisco: HarperSanFrancisco, 1988); Elsa Tamez, *The Scandalous Message of James: Faith without Works Is Dead*, rev. ed. (New York: Crossroad, 2002); and Lyle D. Vander Broek, *Breaking Barriers: The Possibilities of Christian Community in a Lonely World* (Grand Rapids: Brazos, 2002), on 1 Corinthians.

8. See esp. James Callahan, *The Clarity of Scripture: History, Theology, and Contemporary Literary Studies* (Downers Grove, Ill.: InterVarsity Press, 2001).

9. Theophilus may have been either a "seeker" or a new Christian, but the churches that first received Luke's Gospel clearly believed it had value for believers after conversion and not just for people coming to Christ. In John the tense of the verb translated "believe" varies in the manuscripts, so that we are not sure if John meant first-time belief, growth in faith, or (most likely) both.

10. See further Craig L. Blomberg, "The Liberation of Illegitimacy: Women and Rulers in Matthew 1–2," *BTB* 21 (1991): 145–50.

11. Of many good treatments of these themes, see now esp. D. Brent Sandy, *Plowshares and Pruning Hooks: Rethinking the Language of Biblical Prophecy and Apocalyptic* (Downers Grove, Ill.: InterVarsity Press, 2002).

12. Very little evangelical exposition of the New Testament teachings about John the Baptist occurs, even though we know more about him than about any of the other characters from the Gospels besides Jesus himself. From a contemporary Catholic perspective, much of C. R. Kaz-

mierski (*John the Baptist: Prophet and Evangelist* [Collegeville, Minn.: Liturgical, 1996]) proves helpful.

13. For an excellent survey of the diverse forms these vocations can take, both in the Gospels and today, see Scot McKnight, *Turning to Jesus: The Sociology of Conversion in the Gospels* (Louisville: Westminster John Knox Press, 2002).

14. See D. A. Carson, *The Gospel according to John* (Grand Rapids: Eerdmans, 1991), 505.

15. John R. W. Stott (*Christian Counter-Culture: The Message of the Sermon on the Mount* [Downers Grove, Ill.: InterVarsity Press, 1978], 89) elaborates: "That is, don't look! Behave as if you had actually plucked out your eyes and flung them away, and were now blind and so *could* not see the objects which previously caused you to sin."

16. See esp. Robert C. Tannehill, "The 'Focal Instance' as a Form of New Testament Speech: A Study of Matthew 5:39b–42," *JR* 50 (1970): 372–85.

17. See further Stephen C. Barton, *Discipleship and Family Ties in Mark and Matthew* (Cambridge: Cambridge University Press, 1994), 67–96. For incisive contemporary application, see Rodney Clapp, *Families at the Crossroads: Beyond Traditional and Modern Options* (Downers Grove, Ill.: InterVarsity Press, 1993).

18. See D. A. Carson, *The Sermon on the Mount: An Evangelical Exposition of Matthew 5–7* (Grand Rapids: Baker, 1978), 98–99.

19. See further J. Carl Laney, *A Guide to Church Discipline* (Minneapolis: Bethany, 1985); and John White and Ken Blue, *Healing the Wounded: The Costly Love of Church Discipline* (Downers Grove, Ill.: InterVarsity Press, 1985).

20. The best evangelical study of Jesus' miracles now available is Graham H. Twelftree, *Jesus the Miracle Worker* (Downers Grove, Ill.: InterVarsity Press, 1999).

21. On which, see now esp. Marion C. Moeser, *The Anecdote in Mark, the Classical World, and the Rabbis* (London: Sheffield Academic Press, 2002).

22. See esp. William Barclay, *The Plain Man's Guide to Ethics* (Glasgow: Collins, 1973), 26–48. For the larger exegetical, theological, and historical issues at stake, see D. A. Carson, ed., *From Sabbath to Lord's Day* (Grand Rapids: Zondervan, 1982).

23. Craig L. Blomberg, *Interpreting the Parables* (Downers Grove, Ill.: InterVarsity Press, 1990).

24. See further Craig L. Blomberg, *Preaching the Parables* (Grand Rapids: Baker, forthcoming).

25. These applications are well elaborated throughout David E. Garland, *Mark* (Grand Rapids: Zondervan, 1996).

26. See esp. Brent Kinman, "Jesus' Triumphal Entry in the Light of Pilate's," *NTS* 40 (1994): 442–48; and Paul B. Duff, "The March of the Divine Warrior and the Advent of the Greco-Roman King," *JBL* 111 (1992): 55–71.

27. Borrowing the delightful pun from Ben Witherington III, *The Christology of Jesus* (Minneapolis: Fortress, 1990), 107.

28. At the popular level, see esp. Tom Hovestol, *Extreme Righteousness: Seeing Ourselves in the Pharisees* (Chicago: Moody, 1997).

29. By far the fullest treatment of this literature now available is John J. Collins, ed., *The Encyclopedia of Apocalypticism*, 3 vols. (New York: Continuum, 1998). On a popular level, see esp. B. J. Oropeza, *Ninety-nine Reasons Why No One Knows When Christ Will Return* (Downers Grove, Ill.: InterVarsity Press, 1994).

30. See esp. Timothy J. Geddert, *Watchwords: Mark 13 in Markan Eschatology* (Sheffield, England: JSOT, 1989).

31. See the survey of remarkable approaches taken throughout history in Arthur W. Wainwright, *Mysterious Apocalypse* (Nashville: Abingdon, 1993).

32. Insightful and provocative applications appear in Donald Bridge and David Phypers, *The Meal That Unites?* (London: Hodder & Stoughton, 1981).

33. For a thorough discussion of the issues, see John C. Thomas, *Footwashing in John 13 and the Johannine Community* (Sheffield, England: JSOT, 1991).

34. On the correct punctuation of this passage, see John W. Wenham, "When Were the Saints Raised?" *JTS* 32 (1981): 150–52.

35. See further Craig L. Blomberg, "The Globalization of Biblical Interpretation—A Test Case: John 3–4," *BBR* 5 (1995): 1–15.

36. Albert Vanhoye, "La composition de Jean 5,19–30," in *Mélanges Bibliques en hommage au R. P. Béda Rigaux*, ed. Albert Descamps and André de Halleux (Gembloux, France: Duculot, 1970), 259–74.

37. A modification of the outline suggested by Wayne Brouwer, *The Literary Development of John 13–17: A Chiastic Reading* (Atlanta: Scholars, 2000).

38. The definitive study of this text from this perspective was Peder Borgen, *Bread from Heaven* (Leiden: Brill, 1965). The form also appears in miniature with several of the Synoptic parables. The fullest set of suggestions of New Testament texts adopting this form appears scattered

throughout E. Earle Ellis, *The Making of the New Testament Documents* (Leiden: Brill, 2002).

39. The language in these last three sentences has been borrowed from Craig L. Blomberg, *The Historical Reliability of John's Gospel: Issues and Commentary* (Downers Grove, Ill.: InterVarsity Press, 2001), 127.

40. See esp. D. A. Carson, *The Gospel according to John* (Grand Rapids: Eerdmans, 1991), 514–15.

41. See the incisive exposition in Bruce Milne, *The Message of John: Here Is Your King!* (Downers Grove, Ill.: InterVarsity Press, 1993), 247–52.

42. See, e.g., David J. Williams, *Acts* (San Francisco: Harper & Row, 1985), 17.

43. See esp. William J. Larkin, Jr., *Acts* (Downers Grove, Ill.: InterVarsity Press, 1995), 82–83.

44. See esp. Walter L. Liefeld, *Interpreting the Book of Acts* (Grand Rapids: Baker, 1995), 117–27.

45. See further Craig L. Blomberg, *Neither Poverty nor Riches: A Biblical Theology of Material Possessions* (Leicester, England: InterVarsity Press, 1999), 161–71.

46. Some would add a second apparent exception—the experience of the followers of John the Baptist in Ephesus (Acts 19:1–10). These individuals are called "disciples," but as Paul interviews them they claim not even to have heard of the Holy Spirit. This means that they knew very little of John's or Jesus' ministries, given the central role the Spirit played in both. It means they could not have been Jews, since then they would have known of the Spirit from the Hebrew Scriptures. With so little information, it is hard to believe that their discipleship amounted to true, saving faith.

47. See esp. the treatment of this passage in James D. G. Dunn, *Baptism in the Holy Spirit* (Philadelphia: Westminster, 1970), 55–72.

48. See esp. Orlando E. Costas, *Liberating News: A Theology of Contextual Evangelization* (Grand Rapids: Eerdmans, 1989).

49. See esp. C. H. Dodd, *The Apostolic Preaching and Its Developments* (New York: Harper, 1951).

50. See Philip H. Towner, "Mission Practice and Theology under Construction," in *Witness to the Gospel: The Theology of Acts*, ed. I. Howard Marshall and David Peterson (Grand Rapids: Eerdmans, 1998), 417–36.

51. Kenneth Gangel, "Paul's Areopagus Speech," *BSac* 127 (1970): 312. Cf. J. Daryl Charles, "Engaging the (Neo) Pagan Mind: Paul's Encounter with Athenian Culture as a Model for Cultural Apologetics (Acts 17:16–34)," *TrinJ* 16 (1995): 47–62.

52. See esp. Martin Hengel, *Between Jesus and Paul* (Philadelphia: Fortress, 1983), 1–29.

53. See Ronald D. Witherup, "Cornelius Over and Over and Over Again: Functional Redundancy in the Acts of the Apostles," *JSNT* 49 (1993): 45–66.

54. See, respectively, James Smith, *The Voyage and Shipwreck of St. Paul*, 4th ed. (Minneapolis: James Family Christian Publishers, 1880); and Richard I. Pervo, *Profit with Delight: The Literary Genre of the Acts of the Apostles* (Philadelphia: Fortress, 1987), esp. 51–54. Unfortunately and unnecessarily, as with Pervo, who deals with the artistry and adventure of Acts brilliantly, too often the literary is pitted against the historical.

55. The one possible exception is Ephesians, if it is understood as an "encyclical." See the standard New Testament introductions.

56. See, e.g., Douglas J. Moo, *The Epistle to the Romans* (Grand Rapids: Eerdmans, 1996), 786: "Paul does not want Christians to use the inevitability of tension with the world as an excuse for behavior that needlessly exacerbates that conflict or for a resignation that leads us not even to bother to seek to maintain a positive witness."

57. The reverse is less likely the case, since first-time readers would not have known of the later text when encountering the former.

58. See further Craig L. Blomberg, "Neither Hierarchicalist nor Egalitarian: Gender Roles in Paul," in *Two Views on Women in Ministry*, ed. James R. Beck and Craig L. Blomberg (Grand Rapids: Zondervan, 2001), 350–52.

59. See further Craig L. Blomberg, *1 Corinthians* (Grand Rapids: Zondervan, 1994), 207–20.

60. Ibid., 213–14; Blomberg, "Neither Hierarchicalist nor Egalitarian," 347.

61. See further Blomberg, *1 Corinthians*, 150–58.

62. Outstanding practical application appears in Philip Yancey, *What's So Amazing about Grace?* (Grand Rapids: Zondervan, 1997).

63. Blomberg, "Neither Hierarchicalist nor Egalitarian," 357–70.

64. Points made convincingly throughout Stephen F. Miletic, *"One Flesh": Ephesians 5.22–24, 5.31—Marriage and the New Creation* (Rome: Biblical Institute Press, 1988).

65. Thus Moo, *Romans*, 33. Older commentators often divided 1:18–3:20 into two parts, with either 1:18–32 or 1:18–2:16 addressed primarily to Gentiles and 2:1–3:20 or 2:17–3:20 addressed primarily to Jews. The universality of sin, however, remains clear in any of these outlines.

66. E.g., the NIV. But note that the TNIV replaces "no food," with "nothing," adopting a more literal rendering.

67. See further Blomberg, *1 Corinthians*, 202–6. On applying the principle of freedom from legalism more generally, see esp. Charles R. Swindoll, *The Grace Awakening* (Nashville: Word, 1991); Chap Clark, *The Performance Illusion* (Colorado Springs, Colo.: NavPress, 1993).

68. See, e.g., Gary Friesen with J. Robin Maxson, *Decision-Making and the Will of God* (Portland, Oreg.: Multnomah, 1980), 382–83.

69. For excellent application of 1 Corinthians 14 to a variety of settings, see D. A. Carson, *Showing the Spirit: A Theological Exposition of 1 Corinthians 12–14* (Grand Rapids: Baker, 1987), 77–136. For a balanced, biblical theology of spiritual gifts more generally, see Michael Green, *I Believe in the Holy Spirit* (Grand Rapids: Eerdmans, 1975), 161–96.

70. See esp. Harold W. Hoehner, *Ephesians: An Exegetical Commentary* (Grand Rapids: Baker, 2002), 720–29.

71. See further Blomberg, *Neither Poverty nor Riches*, 190–99. Cf. Ronald J. Sider, *Rich Christians in an Age of Hunger*, 4th ed. (Dallas: Word, 1997), 193–96.

72. Because of the unique features applying only to Christ, some have disputed that the hymn is meant to function in an exemplary role at all. But this swings the pendulum too far in the opposite direction. For a full history of interpretation, with balanced conclusions, see Ralph P. Martin, *A Hymn of Christ: Philippians 2:5–11 in Recent Interpretation and in the Setting of Early Christian Worship* (Downers Grove, Ill.: InterVarsity Press, 1997).

73. See Loveday Alexander, "Hellenistic Letter Forms and the Structure of Philippians," *JSNT* 37 (1989): 87–101.

74. See further Robert Jewett, *Christian Tolerance* (Philadelphia: Westminster, 1982).

75. See esp. D. A. Carson, "Pauline Inconsistency: Reflections on 1 Corinthians 9.19–23 and Galatians 2.11–14," *Churchman* 100 (1986): 6–45.

76. F. F. Bruce, *Paul: Apostle of the Heart Set Free* (Grand Rapids: Eerdmans, 1977), 401.

77. See esp. Willard Swartley, *Slavery, Sabbath, War, and Women* (Scottdale, Pa.: Herald, 1983). More recently, in an important study of three partially parallel and highly controversial issues, William J. Webb (*Slaves, Women, and Homosexuals: Exploring the Hermeneutics of Cultural Analysis* [Downers Grove, Ill.: InterVarsity Press, 2001]) develops what he calls a "redemptive movement" hermeneutic. The heart of his argument is that just as one can trace developing understanding of various topics within successive stages of Old Testament revelation as well as from the Old

Testament to the New, so also there may be places where the "trajectory" of biblical thought implies that Christians today should move beyond NT teaching. Webb believes Christians have already properly done this on the issue of slavery. He convincingly shows that the biblical data on homosexuality do *not* fit such a trajectory. Homosexual practice is equally condemned throughout both Testaments. But he believes biblical teaching on women is more akin to that on slavery. He does not interpret biblical teaching on gender roles as promoting egalitarianism as biblical feminists do, but he does see development of thought moving in a direction that would support Christians today going beyond the New Testament to support complete interchangeability of gender roles in home and church. Much of Webb's work proves persuasive, but a few nagging questions remain. There really is no biblical text on gender roles analogous to 1 Cor. 7:21, encouraging women to become elders or heads over their husbands if the opportunity arises. If one interprets the key texts regarding gender roles as affirming complementarianism rather than egalitarianism in Paul's world, then it is difficult to see where the trajectory of development appears *within* the New Testament to justify further movement in a direction that later goes explicitly beyond the New Testament.

78. See esp. Ben Witherington III, "Rite and Rights for Women—Gal. 3.28," *NTS* 27 (1981): 593–94.

79. See further Blomberg, "Diversity of Literary Genres," 283–85.

80. All these generalizations are intentionally designed to be broad enough that Arminians and Calvinists alike can agree on them. For a compelling reconstruction of what life might have been like for one Jewish Christian young person in Rome at this time, written as a piece of historical fiction, see George H. Guthrie, *Hebrews* (Grand Rapids: Zondervan, 1998), 17–18.

81. Although her claims occasionally go beyond the text itself, Tamez (*James*) engages in a close reading of James from a Latin American liberationist perspective with which every middle-class Western Christian should have to come to grips.

82. See, respectively, John H. Elliott, *A Home for the Homeless: A Sociological Exegesis of 1 Peter, Its Situation and Strategy* (Philadelphia: Fortress, 1981); and Bruce W. Winter, *Seek the Welfare of the City: Christians as Benefactors and Citizens* (Grand Rapids: Eerdmans, 1994). Winter has an important treatment of 1 Peter but also considers significant Pauline material.

83. For these and related themes, see esp. Richard Bauckham, *The Theology of the Book of Revelation* (Cambridge: Cambridge University Press, 1993).

84. See now esp. Grant R. Osborne, *Revelation* (Grand Rapids: Baker, 2002).

85. For a fascinating study of Christian speculation on the Antichrist throughout church history, see Bernard McGinn, *Antichrist: Two Thousand Years of the Human Fascination with Evil* (San Francisco: HarperSanFrancisco, 1994).

86. For helpful comparisons of the millennial positions, see Robert G. Clouse, ed., *The Meaning of the Millennium: Four Views* (Downers Grove, Ill.: InterVarsity Press, 1977); on the tribulation, see Richard Reiter, ed., *The Rapture and the Tribulation: Pre-, Mid-, or Post-tribulational* (Grand Rapids: Zondervan, 1984). For four approaches to Revelation as a whole, expounded passage by passage, see C. Marvin Pate, ed., *Four Views on the Book of Revelation* (Grand Rapids: Zondervan, 1998), with preterist, idealist, and two different futurist perspectives presented.

87. Printed bibliographies of key resources quickly go out of date. But see the Old and New Testament departmental bibliographies, updated twice annually, in the *Denver Journal,* an online publication of book reviews, accessible from the home page of Denver Seminary's website (www.denverseminary.edu). Two excellent bibliographies have, however, been published recently: John Glynn, *Commentary and Reference Survey,* rev. ed. (Grand Rapids: Kregel, 2003); and David R. Bauer, *An Annotated Guide to Biblical Resources for Ministry* (Peabody, Mass.: Hendrickson, 2003).

Subject Index

Abba (Father), 100, 101
Acrocorinth, 56
Acts, Book of
  application of, 126–31
  archaeological evidence and,
    56–57
  characterization of Paul, 42–43
  dating of, 26
  genre of, 28–31
  historical content of, 50–53
  speeches in, 30–31, 129–30,
    155 n. 73
Acts Seminar, 19
Agabus, 32
Agapius, 47
Alexander, Loveday, 28
Alexander the Great, 27–28, 38
Allison, Dale, 106
amēn ("truly"), 100
Ananias, 105, 127
Annas, 41, 50
Antipas, 50
Antonia Fortress, 53
apocalyptic literature, 119–20, 142
apocryphal Acts, 25
apocryphal Gospels, 24
Apollonius, 66
Apollonius of Tyana, 67
Apostolic Council (Acts 15), 45,
  131

Apostolic Fathers, as literature,
  59–60
Appian, 38
Aratus, 52
Archko Volume, The, 17
Areopagus, 57, 156 n. 83
Arrian, 27–28
Artemis, 56
Artemis cult, 57
Asclepius, 67
Asia Minor, 142
Asnius Pollio, 38
Athens, 51, 57, 129
Augustine, 37
Augustus, 50

Barclay, John, 96
Barnabas, 51, 56, 59
Bartimaeus, 38–39
basileia (Gk., "kingdom"), 89
Baur, Ferdinand Christian, 71
Beale, Greg, 60
Bethsaida, 54
Bible Speaks Today, 109
biography, genre of, 30
"bread from heaven," 124
Bread of Life, as term for Jesus,
  124
Bruce, F. F., 72, 90, 140
Bultmann, Rudolf, 65, 72

Caesarea Maritimis, 54
Caiaphas, 41, 50, 54
Capernaum, 53
Capernaum synagogue, 124
Celsus, 49
Cerinthus, 40
chiasmus, 122–23
"Christ," as term for Jesus, 101–2
Christ hymn (Phil. 2:5–11), 81,
    138, 172 n. 72
Christian creeds, 63–65
Christianity, books about, 17–19
Christian prophecy, history of,
    31–32
Church of the Holy Sepulchre
    (Jerusalem), 54
circumcision, 45
Claudius, 49, 51
Clement, 59
Colossae, 57
Constantine, 93
corban ("dedicated to God"), 55
Corinth, 45, 46, 51, 56–57, 72
Cornelius, 131
"creation ordinances," 134–35

Damascus, 105
Damascus Road experience
    (Paul), 84, 104, 146
Day of Preparation, 37
Dead Sea Scrolls, 18
Death of Pergrinus, The (Lucian of
    Samosata), 49
Derbe, 56
Didache, 59
dietary laws, 76, 93–94, 136
dikaiosunē (Gk., "justification"),
    89, 163 n. 54
Diogenes Laertius, 30
dissimilarity criterion, 20, 68
divorce, New Testament teaching
    on, 45–46, 75
Dodd, C. H., 85

Ehrman, Bart, 33
ekklēsia (Gk., "church"), 94

Emmaus, 58
Epaphroditus, 138
Ephesus, 40, 51, 56, 57, 170 n. 46
Epimenides, 52
epistles, genre of, 86
Erastus, 57
Essene sect (Qumran), 32
Eucharist, 62, 96. *See also* Last
    Supper, "words of institution"

Farewell Discourse (Jesus), 112,
    123–24
First Corinthians, 61, 62–63
First Peter, 60, 141–42
First Thessalonians, 61, 63
foot-washing, 121
Fraser, J. W., 72
Freitag, Jeanette, 11

Gadara, province of, 37
Galatia, 51
Gallic War (Caesar), 22
Gallio, 51, 56
Gallio inscription, 56
Gangel, Kenneth, 130
General Epistles, application of,
    140–42, 147
"Gentile Pentecost," 131
Gerasa, 37
Golgotha, 54
Gordon's Calvary (Jerusalem), 54
Gospel of Thomas, 19, 149–50 n. 5
Gospels
    application of, 109–26
    archaeological evidence and,
        53–56
    dating of, 145
    discrepancies among, 36–42
    genre of, 28–31, 145
    harmonization in, 37–39
    historical accuracy of, 20–21,
        145
    literary forms in, 146
    scholarship on, 20–21
    textual sources for, 27
    titles of, 24

Goulder, Michael, 72
Great Commission (Matt. 28:19), 112

Hanina ben Dosa, 66, 67
Harmony of the Gospels (Augustine), 37
Harrelson, Jeremiah, 11
Hebrews, Book of, 141, 147
Hegel, G. W. F., 71
"Hellenists," as word, 52
Hemer, Colin, 50
Hengel, Martin, 151 n. 18
Hermes, 51
Herod Agrippa I, 50, 51
Herod Agrippa II, 50
Herodotus, 28
Herod's palace, 155 n. 76
Herod the Great, 50
Hierapolis, 58
hilastērion (Gk., atoning sacrifice), 90
history, harmonization in, 37–39
Holy Communion. *See* Last Supper
Holy Spirit, 112, 126, 128
homosexuality, 172–73 n. 77
Honi the Rain-maker, 66, 67
Hume, David, 65–66
hupokritēs (Gk., "hypocrite"), 55

Ignatius, 59
Iliad (Homer), 34
Irenaeus, 26
Islam, 151 n. 17

Jacob's well (Sychar), 53
Jaffa Gate (Jerusalem), 155 n. 76
James, Book of, 60–61, 141
James, brother of Jesus, 47, 54
Jericho, 38
"Jesus boat," the, 54
Jesus Christ
    apocalyptic discourse, 120
    baptism of, 98
    birth narratives concerning, 111

church origins and, 94–96
creeds concerning, 64–65
divine attributes of, 44
genealogy of, 110
Gentile mission and, 95–96
"hard sayings" of, 43–44
Jewish Law and, 76
messianic status of, 98, 101–2, 105, 115, 119
miracles of, 115–16
New Testament portraits of, 13–14
Old Testament Law and, 91–94, 130, 146
oral traditions and, 62–63, 64
parables of, 117–18
"Paschal" sacrifice, 93
Passion predictions of, 103, 120–21
references in Pauline writings, 73–81
resurrection of, 64–65, 68–70, 86–87, 103–4, 105, 121–22
symbolic actions, 118–19
teachings to disciples, 112–15
temptations of, 111–12
women and, 96–97
Jesus Seminar, 19, 76, 88, 150 n. 7
Jewish Antiquities (Josephus), 47
Jewish Christianity, 64, 69, 141
Jewish literature, 46, 155 n. 74. *See also* Talmud
Johannine epistles, 86
John, as author, 25
John, Gospel of
    composition of, 40–41
    distinctiveness of, 29
    Gnosticism and, 40–41
    historical reliability of, 152 n. 31
    relationship with Synoptic Gospels, 164 n. 66
    textual sources for, 152 n. 32
John the Baptist, 39, 50, 99, 111, 167–68 n. 12, 170 n. 46
Josephus, 28, 38, 47–48, 50, 58

Judas, 126
Julius Africanus, 49
Julius Caesar, 37
justification by faith (Pauline),
    88–91, 134, 146

Khersa, 37, 53
Kim, Seyoon, 104
kingdom of God (Pauline), 89–91
kurios (Gk.), 102

Laodicea, 57, 58
Last Supper, 37, 62, 73–74, 99, 121
"Law of Christ," 92
"Lives of the Philosophers" (Dio-
    genes Laertius), 30
Livy, 22
Loisy, Alfred, 94
"Lord," as term for Jesus, 102
Lord's Prayer, 89
Lord's Supper. *See* Eucharist
Lucian of Samosata, 49, 158 n. 108
Lüdemann, Gerd, 64–65, 72–73
Luke, as author, 25, 127, 130–31,
    147. *See also* Acts, Book of
Luke, Gospel of, 26, 28–29
Lystra, 51, 56, 129

malkuth (Heb., "kingdom"), 89
Mara bar Serapion, 49
Mark, as author, 24
Mars Hill (Athens), 57, 156 n. 83
"Mars Hill" speech (Paul), 42
Marx, Karl, 71
Mary and Martha of Bethany, 97
Mary Magdalene, 53
Matthew, as author, 25
Matthew, Gospel of
    apocalyptic literature in,
        119–20
    birth narratives in, 111
    genealogies in, 110
    Jesus' teaching in, 112–15
    Jesus' temptations in, 111–12
    John the Baptist and, 111
    miracles stories in, 115–16

parables in, 117–18
Passion narratives in, 120–21
proverbs and pronounce-
    ments, 116–17
resurrection narratives in,
    121–22
textual sources for, 61
Meier, John, 68
Merkley, Paul, 37
Merz, Annette, 21
"Messiah," as term for Jesus,
    101–2
Middle East
    head-coverings in, 133
    memorization customs in, 35
    oral cultures in, 34–35
miracle stories (Gospel of John),
    27
miracles. *See* New Testament,
    miracle stories in
missionary discourses, 160 n. 19
Mnason, 52
Moon, Lottie, 134
Mormonism, 151 n. 17
Moses, 83
"Moses' seat," 53
Moule, C. F. D., 85
"Mount of Beatitudes," 54
Mount of Olives, 55
Mount of Transfiguration, 83
Mount Sinai, 83
Mount Zion, 54
"multiple attestation," 20

natural theology, 42
Nazi holocaust, 32–33
Nazirite, 133
New Testament
    archaeology and, 53–58
    authorship of, 23–25
    Christian creeds in, 63–65
    dating of, 25–28
    genres of, 108
    literary forms in, 108
    manuscript evidence for, 22–23
    miracle stories in, 65–70

"pre-formed traditions" in, 154 n. 58
New Testament apocrypha, 151 n. 20
New Testament Commentary Series, InterVarsity Press, 109
Nicodemus, 122
Nietzsche, Friedrich, 71
NIV Application Commentaries, 108–9

Odyssey (Homer), 34
Old Testament Law, 91–94. See also Jesus Christ, Old Testament Law and; Paul, Old Testament Law and
Olivet Discourse (Mark 13), 63, 77, 78
Onesimus, 140
Origen, 48, 49
Oxford papyrus (Gospel of Matthew), 18

pacifism, 132
Palm Sunday, 98
Papias, 24, 25, 59, 156 n. 88
parable of the good Samaritan (Luke 10:25–37), 117
parable of the Pharisee and the tax collector (Luke 18:9–14), 90, 117–18
parable of the thief, 63
"Paraclete" (Holy Spirit), 112, 123
Passion narratives, 120–21
"passion prediction" (Mark 8:31; 9:31; 10:33–34), 103
Passover festival, 37
Pastoral Epistles, 164–65 n. 79
Paul
    christology of, 97–102
    concern for poor, 83
    conversion of, 104–5, 146
    "domestic codes" and, 137–38
    eschatological thought in, 76–78, 103–4
    food sacrifices and, 136–37

Gentile mission and, 94–96, 160 n. 18
    historical treatments of, 20
    Jesus traditions and, 84–88, 146, 161 n. 34
    knowledge of Gospel tradition, 81–82
    Old Testament Law and, 91–94, 134–35, 146
    Petrine Christianity and, 71–73
    portrayals in Acts and epistles, 42–43
    slavery and, 140
    statements on marriage, 133–34
    theology of, 88–91
    third use of the Law, 91–92
    voyage and shipwreck, 131
    women and, 96–97, 132, 164–65 n. 79
Pauline epistles
    application of, 131–40
    authorship of, 162–63 n. 53
    textual sources for, 61–63
    See also Paul
Pergamum, 57
"perspicuity" of Scripture, 109
Peter, 71, 118, 119, 129, 131
Philemon, Book of, 140
Philippi, 56
Philippians, Book of, 138–39
philosophy of science, 66–67
Phrygia, 51
Pisidian Antioch, 52, 56
Pliny the Younger, 49
Plutarch, 27, 38
Pontius Pilate, 41, 50, 54
pool of Bethesda, 53
pool of Siloam, 53
Porter, Stanley, 81–82
proem midrash, 124
"pronouncement stories" (Gospels), 116

"Q" source, 151 n. 24
qāhāl (Heb., "assembly"), 94

Quirinius, 58
Qumran, 18

Rabbi Abbahu, 49
resurrection, belief in, 68–70. *See also* Jesus Christ, resurrection of
Resurrection of the Son of God, The (Wright), 68
Revelation, Book of
    application of, 142–43
    archaeological evidence and, 57–58
    textual sources for, 60
Rhoda, 52
Romans, Book of, 61–62, 139
Rubicon River, 37

Sabbath commandment, 92–93, 116–17
Samaritans, 128
Samaritan woman, 122
Sapphira, 127
Sepphoris, 55
Sergius Paulus, 56
Sermon on the Mount, 54–55, 59, 61, 75, 76, 91, 92, 112
Shaw, George Bernard, 71
Sheep Gate (Jerusalem), 53
"Shepherd of Hermas," 59
Sherwin-White, A. N., 28
Shroud of Turin, 55–56
"signs source," 27
Simon the Magician, 128–29
Simon the Zealot, 25
Smith, Joseph, 23
Smyrna, 57
"Son of David," as term for Jesus, 102
"Son of Man," as term for Jesus, 101
speaking in tongues, 45
spermologos, term for Paul, 80
"stations of the cross," 155 n. 76
Stephen, 130

Stinson, Michelle, 11
Stoa (Athens), 156 n. 83
Stott, John, 134
Strauss, David, 66
Stunkel, June, 12
Suetonius, 38, 49
Synagogue of the Freedmen (Jerusalem), 51
Synoptic Apocalypse (Mark 13), 77–78
Synoptic Gospels
    differences among, 38–39
    "explicit christology" of, 101–2
    "implicit christology" of, 98–100, 146
    Jesus' teaching in, 95
    Last Supper and, 73–74
    relationship with Gospel of John, 39–42
    textual sources of, 160 n. 22

Tacitus, 22, 49
Talmud, Jesus traditions in, 48–49
"Teacher of Righteousness" (Qumran), 35
Ten Commandments, 92–93
tertius usus legis (Paul's third use of the Law), 91–92
Tertullus, 52
textual criticism, 21–23, 150–51 n. 16
Thallus, 49
Theissen, Gerd, 21
Theophilus, 109, 167 n. 9
Thessalonica, 56
Theudas, 58
Thiede, Carsten, 18
Thiering, Barbara, 18
Third Quest for the historical Jesus, 19–20
Thucydides, 28
Thyatira, 57
Tiberias, 55
Tiberius, 54

Timothy, 138
Trajan, 49
Tyrannus, 52

Universal History (Agapius), 47

Velleius Paterculus, 38
Via Dolorosa, 155 n. 76
Vielhauer, Phillip, 42

Webb, William J., 172–73 n. 77

Wedderburn, Alexander J. M., 96
Wenham, David, 43, 72, 96
Winter, Dagmar, 21
Witherington, Ben, 19–20, 89
"words of institution" (Eucharist), 62, 99, 121
Wrede, William, 71
Wright, N. T., 20–21, 68

Zechariah, 118–19
Zeus, 51

Scripture Index

Exodus
3:14 124
20 92
20:8–11 69

Leviticus
12:8 83
19:18 80

Numbers
6 133

Deuteronomy
21:23 70

Psalms
2:7 98
90:4 32

Isaiah
6:9–10 40
40:3 39
42:1 98

Daniel
7:13 101
7:13–14 60
12:2 103, 121

Joel
2:1 32

Obadiah
14 32

Habakkuk
2:3 32

Zechariah
9:9 98, 118–19

Matthew
1:1–17 110
1:18–2:23 111
3 111
3:7 82
3:13–16 111
4:1–11 82, 111
4:12–7:29 112
4:18–22 112
5–7 61
5:11–12 61
5:13–16 89
5:17–20 91
5:21–48 92
5:25–26 95
5:29 113
5:33 95
5:37 81
5:38 75
5:39 61, 95
5:41 95
5:44 75, 95

5:48 61
5:49 113
6:1 113
6:3 113
6:4 113
6:10 89, 115
7:1 76, 114
7:1–2a 62
7:3–5 114
7:7 61
7:7–11 115
8–9 115
8:5 36
8:27 115
8:28 37
9:1–8 115
9:4–6 116
9:12 116
10:5–6 112
10:9–12 112
10:10 62, 74
10:19–20 120
10:32–33 100
10:37 44, 113–14
11:11 99
11:25–27 79
12:1–8 116
12:8 116
12:9–13 116
12:13 116
12:24 48

183

12:28 98, 115
12:38–39 83
12:41–42 99
13:1–52 117
14:28 102
16:13–20 118
16:17 79
16:18 94
16:21–28 118
16:24 118
16:24–27 121
17:20 79
18:15–17 79
18:15–20 114, 115
18:17 94
18:21–22 114
18:23–35 114
19:1–12 134
19:10–12 75
19:16 91
19:23 91
19:24 91
19:25 91
19:28 99
20:29 38
20:30–34 38
21:1–11 119
21:16 100
21:21 61, 78
21:28 119
22:14 119
22:40 80
23 55, 77
23:1–36 119
23:4 119
23:5 119
23:7 119
23:8 119
23:10 119
23:27 55
23:29–38 63
23:32 77
23:32–36 77

23:34–35 77
23:36 77
23:39 104
24–25 77, 119
24:3 120
24:6 120
24:31 77
24:37–42 78
24:43 63
24:43–44 78
24:43–25:46 120
25:1–13 78
25:31–46 104, 110
26–27 120
26:17–30 121
26:52–54 120
26:62 120
27:51–53 103, 121
28:19 112
28:20 111

Mark
1:9–11 82
1:16–20 42
2:1–12 100
2:27 93
3:4 93
3:31–35 96, 114
4:3–9 80
4:10–12 124
5:1 37
5:34 90
6:5–6 44
6:14–29 41
7:9–13 93
7:10 44
7:14–22 93
7:18–19 76
7:19b 62, 94
7:24–8:10 95
8:11–13 83
8:29 102
8:31 103

8:38 100, 110
9:1 84
9:2 83
9:31 103
10:1–12 45, 95
10:2–12 75
10:7 75
10:33–34 103
10:45 76, 81, 103
10:46 38
10:52 90
11:1–11 98
11:12–25 119
11:15–19 98
11:23 61
11:23–24 78
12:13–17 95
12:17 62, 76
12:31 62
12:35–37 102
13 63, 77, 104
13:2 93, 99
13:8 78
13:9–11 95
13:14–20 78
13:26 77
13:27 77
13:32 44
13:33 78
14:12–16 37
14:22 96
14:24 99
14:32 100
14:38 80
14:53–65 41
14:62 102
15 45
15:1–3 41
16:9–20 23

Luke
1:1–4 28
1:2–2:52 111

1:4 110
2:1 50, 58
2:24 83
3:10–14 111
3:23–37 110
5:8 102
6:20–49 61
6:23 61
6:27 75
6:27b–28a 61
6:28 75
6:36 75
6:37 76
7:6 36
7:50 90
8:1–3 83, 97
8:26 37
9:57–58 83
9:57–62 114
10 160 n. 18
10:7 62, 74, 76
10:8 76
10:16 79
10:21–22 79
10:25–37 117
10:39 97
10:41–42 97
11:9 61
11:15 48
11:41 62
11:48–51 77
12:8–9 100
12:32 96
12:35–38 78
12:39 63
12:39–40 78
14:26 44, 93
15:3–7 96, 100
15:8–10 100
15:11–32 100
17:19 90
18:9–14 117
18:14 90

18:35 38
21 77
22:19–20 62, 73
22:35–38 112
23:8–9 83

John
1:35–42 42
2:12–25 164 n. 66
2:19 93
3 122
3:3 60, 90
3:5 90
3:24 41
4 122
4:48 83
5:19–30 122
5:24 123
5:24–25 123
5:25 123
5:28–29 110
6:25–59 124
6:31 124
6:31–58 124
6:32–40 124
6:39–40 125
6:41–44 124
6:45–47 124
6:48–58 124
7:14–52 124
7:40–52 124
7:53–8:11 23
8:12 60
8:30–31 124
8:31–59 124
8:58 124
8:59 124
10:29 125
13:2–17 121
13:23–25 25
14:1 123
14–16 123
14:2–14 123

14:15–21 123
14:22–31 123
14:26 29, 112
15:1–8 123
15:1–17 123
15:2 125
15:9–17 86, 123
15:18–16:4 123
16:5–16 123
16:17–32 123
16:33 123
17:20 125
17:20–23 125
17:23 125
18:13 41
18:19–23 41
18:24 41
18:28 37, 41
18:31 42
18:31–33 22
18:36 90
18:37–38 22
19:13 53
19:14 37
19:26–27 25
19:35 29
19:34–35 25
20:2–5 25
20:8 25
20:29 60
20:31 29, 110
21:1–7 25
21:20–22 25
21:24 29

Acts
1:1–2 28
1:26 126
2:38–39 128
2:42 73
2:42–47 127
2:46–47 127
3:12–26 31

4:6 50
4:12 128
4:32–5:11 127
5:1–11 127
5:2–4 127
5:9 51
5:12–16 127
5:36 58
6:1–7 127
7 126
7:2–53 130
8 35
8:12–17 128
8:13 128
8:20 129
8:21 129
9:1–19 104
9:17–19 105
9:20 105
10 126, 131
10:36–38 85
11:1–18 131
11:27–30 51, 127
11:28 32
12:4 50
12:13–14 52
13–28 56
13:9 52
13:13 25
13:14 52
13:16–41 129
13:16–48 31
13:39 43, 126
14:12 51
14:15–18 31, 129
15 35, 87
15:6–11 131
16:3 42
16:6 51
16:31 128
17:8 56
17:16–33 42
17:16–34 51
17:18 80

17:22–31 129
17:27 43
17:28 52
17:31 43
18:18 42
19:1–10 170 n. 46
19:9–10 52
20:17–35 51, 129
20:28 43
20:35 81
21 35
21–28 26
21:11 32
21:16 52
22:20–36 126
23:34 52
24:2–4 52
25:21 50
25:25 50
27 131
27:13–20 131
27:21–26 131
28:11–13 50

Romans
1–5 89
1:3 82, 102
1:16 96
1:18–32 42, 135, 171
    n. 65
1:18–2:16 171 n. 65
1:18–3:20 135, 171
    n. 65
1:19–20 43
2:1–3:8 135
2:1–3:20 171 n. 65
2:17–3:20 171 n. 65
3:9–20 135
3:21–31 86
3:23 135
3:25 90
4 134
4–7 91
4:24 69

4:25 69, 82
5:6 82
5:8 82
5:15 82
6:1 144
6:4 69
6:9 69
6:17 84
7:21 172 n. 77
8:9 128
8:11 69
8:12–13 80
8:15 101
8:15–16 84
8:34 69, 82
9–11 96
9:5 82, 102
10:9 69, 102
11:25–26 104
12:1–2 139
12–15 75
12:1–15:13 139
12:2 139
12:3–8 139
12:9–13 139
12:9–13:14 139
12:14 61, 75
12:17 61, 75
12:17–21 132
12:18–19 75
13:1–7 132
13:4 132
13:7 62, 75
13:8–9 62
13:8–14 139
13:14 84
14 137, 172 n. 69
14:1–12 137
14:1–15:13 139
14–15 94
14:10 62
14:13 76
14:13–15:4 137
14:14 62, 76, 136

14:17 90
14:39–40 137
15:1–3 76
15:1–4 81
15:1–6 84
15:7–13 137
15:12 82
15:19 68
16:1 97
16:3–16 97
16:7 97
16:23 57

1 Corinthians
1–2 79
1–4 160 n. 26
1:22 82
1:23 82
2:2 42
2:1–4 86
3:1–3 80
3:10–17 104
3:16–17 93
4:20–21 90
5:1–5 79
5–7 57
5:5 79
5:7 93
6:9–10 90
6:14 69
6:16 75
6:19 93
7 74, 159 nn. 13, 14
7:8 93
7:9 134
7:10 74
7:10–11 45, 62
7:12 46, 74
7:21 140
7:25 46, 75
7:25–28 133
7:26 134
7:26–27 93
7:28a 134

7:28 134
7:29 134
7:29–35 134
7:31 134
7:32–35 93, 134
7:36 134
7:38a 134
7:38 93
7:39 134
7:40 46, 75, 93
8 136
8–10 94
8:1–11:1 136
8:11 82
9 87, 92, 159 n. 14
9:5 82
9:14 62, 74, 76
9:19–23 92, 136, 139
9:20 43
9:21 92
10:13 115
10:25–27 137
10:27 76
10:28–29a 137
10:29b–30 137
10:33–11:1 81
11:1 84
11 133
11:2–16 132, 140
11:4–10 133
11:5 132
11:14 133
11:14–16 133
11:15 133
11:16 133
11:23–25 62, 73, 82
11:27 96
11:29 96
12 96
12:1–3 139
12–14 45, 139
12:4–31 139
12:7–11 97
13:1–13 139

13:2 78
14:1–40 139
14:26–40 95
14:33–38 132, 140
14:34 132
14:34–35 164 n. 79
14:35 132
15 43, 69, 103
15:1–58 86
15:3 82
15:4 82
15:3–7 64
15:5–7 82
15:20 103
15:21–28 103
15:23 122
15:35–49 103
15:50 90

2 Corinthians
1:17 81
3:1–4:6 83
3:18 83, 84
4:14 69
5:11–21 86
5:15 69
5:16 72
5:21 82
8–9 83, 137
8:9 83
8:16–9:5 113
10:1 84
10–13 87
12:12 68

Galatians
1:1 69
1 104
1–2 35, 87
1–4 89
1:6–10 139
1:11–12 104, 105,
  146
1:15–16 79

1:18 105
1:18–20 105
1:19 82
2 45
2:2 51
2:9 83
2:10 51
2:11–14 79
3:1 51
3:1–18 134
3–4 42
3:5 68
3:10–14 86
3:19–20 91
3:21–4:7 91
3:28 140
4:4 82
4:6 82, 101
5:13–26 91
5:14 62, 80, 92
5:16–17 80
5:21 90
6:2 92

Ephesians
4:22 107
5:22–24 137
5:22–27 135
5:22–33 140
5:25–28 137
5:24a 135
5:24b 135
5:25a 135
5:25b 135
6:2–3 93
6:5–8 140

Philippians
1:1–11 138
1:12–26 138
1:15–18 139
1:19–26 43
1:21 84
1:27–2:18 138
2:5 138
2:5–11 81, 138

2:6 64, 138
2:6–11 64
2:7 81
2:8 82
2:9 138
2:19–30 138
3:1–4:1 138
3:2–11 139
3:18–19 94
4:2–3 97
4:2–23 138
4:13 107

Colossians
1:5–6 80
1:14–20 80
1:15 64
1:15–20 64
2:16–17 93
3:22–25 140
4:10 90
4:14 25

1 Thessalonians
1:6 80, 84
1:10 69
2:11–12 90
2:13 80
2:14–16 63
2:15 82
2:15–16 76
4:8 79
4:12–5:11 104
4:14 82
4:15 42, 77
4:15–17 63
4:15–5:4 63
4:16a 77
4:16–17 77
4:16b 77
4:16c 77
4:17 77, 160 n. 21
5 77
5:2 77
5:2–4 63
5:3 78

5:4 77
5:4–6 78

2 Thessalonians
1:5–12 90
2:1–12 104
2:3–6 78

1 Timothy
2:8–15 140
2:12 97, 135
2:13 135
3:1–7 135
4:11–16 136
4:13 136
5:8 107
5:17 135

2 Timothy
4:11 25

Philemon
24 25

Hebrews
2:4 68
2:18 111
4:15–16 112

James
1:2 61
1:4 61
1:5 61
1:6 61

1 Peter
1:2 60
1:8 60
2:9 60
3:18–22 64
3:22 64

1 John
2:7–11 86
2:19 125
5:13 125

Revelation
1:3 32
1:4–8 142
1:7 142
2–3 32, 57, 142

2:7 57
2:10 57
2:13 57
2:27 57
3:15 58

3:18 57
3:20 57
4–5 142
6–19 142
20–22 110, 142